Flying Lightning

Flying Lightning

The History of the
14th Fighter Squadron

Dave Thole

Writers Club Press
San Jose New York Lincoln Shanghai

Flying Lightning
The History of the 14th Fighter Squadron

All Rights Reserved © 2001 by Dave Thole

No part of this book may be reproduced or transmitted in any form or by any means, graphic, electronic, or mechanical, including photocopying, recording, taping, or by any information storage retrieval system, without the permission in writing from the publisher.

Writers Club Press
an imprint of iUniverse.com, Inc.

For information address:
iUniverse.com, Inc.
5220 S 16th, Ste. 200
Lincoln, NE 68512
www.iuniverse.com

ISBN: 0-595-19968-2

Printed in the United States of America

To my dad, Lou Thole, who inspired me, encouraged me, and who is, without a doubt, the coolest man on the face of the earth.

Contents

Foreword ix
Introduction xi
Chapter 1: Blue Lightnings and Spitfires
            —The 14th Photographic Reconnaissance Squadron 1
Chapter 2: Jink, Jam, and Chaff
            —The 14th Tactical Reconnaissance Squadron 53
Chapter 3: Vipers in Japan—The 14th Fighter Squadron 117
About the Author 191
Appendix 193
Glossary 201

Foreword

Our combined efforts constitute the foundation for this book. Here is a pictorial representation of the life of our squadron, from its inception to the present time. During this interval we grew from a fledgling outfit into an experienced organization, capable of doing not only a good job, but also the best job of which we are capable, and this we have done. Victory the proof of our efforts, has been realized. This is our part in that victory, both at work and at play. This is the story of the 14th.

Foreword to the 14th Photographic Reconnaissance Squadron (PRS) Yearbook, 1945

Introduction

"Always maintain plenty of speed in a fight, then if you should miss a shot you can pull up for another pass. Never try to turn more than 90 degrees with any enemy plane."

"All new pilots should be briefed in the advantages we have over the enemy and the advantages he has over us. There are speeds and altitudes at which our airplanes can out-turn theirs. Know the limitations of your ship and of the enemy's ship. Complicated tactics will work, but it would take months of practice for which we haven't time."

"Keep your head on a swivel and know what is going on around and behind you. If you see the enemy first, or when they are still a good distance away, you are **never** at a disadvantage."

"Make sure that if you do attack that you are not also being followed. No matter how well you look around you, you will not see all the planes in the area."

"In cases where you are defensive, it doesn't matter much what you do, but do **something** and do it violently!"

Those are some pretty good words of wisdom for today's fighter pilot. Who said all that anyway? Ritchie? DeBellvue? Cunningham? Dano? The answer is none of the above. All of those quotes were taken from a document printed during World War Two (WW II) called *Twelve to One*. It was produced by the Fifth Fighter Command, which during WW II was part of the very same Fifth Air Force to which the 14th Fighter Squadron currently belongs. It is a first-hand account of the tactics and techniques of the pilots flying P-39s, P-40s, P-38s, and P-47s in the southwest Pacific. It was distributed in an effort to pass on some of the hard-learned lessons from the old heads to the new guys.

It's been said that there is nothing new in flying fighters. Granted, certain allowances must be made for new technology. But the basics that kept guys alive in WW II will certainly keep today's fighter pilots coming back to the bar after dropping their bombs and shooting down MiGs. With that in mind, I've produced this history of the mighty 14th Fighter Squadron. If you are looking for facts and figures, you'll have to look somewhere else. Since time does take its toll on the memory, you may find inaccuracies in dates and times and specifications. What you will find, though, are many first-hand accounts of the pilots and weapons system operators (*WSO*s) who were there, flying and fighting in the 14th, from WW II to the present day. Hopefully, this will give today's young hotshot some idea of what it was like in the old days. And it just might give some of the crusty fighter pilots of old a taste of what it is like in the cockpit of the F-16. For those of you who aren't pilots, don't worry. These guys won't bite. Belly up to the bar, order a beer, and enjoy the stories. If you run across a word you don't know, if it's in **bold italics** then you can find a description in the glossary.

Blue Lightnings and Spitfires
—The 14th Photographic Reconnaissance Squadron

The 14th Fighter Squadron, today flying the Lockheed Martin F-16 Fighting Falcon and known as the "Fightin' Samurai," had its genesis in the turbulent days after the bombing of Pearl Harbor. The US military had been keeping a keen eye to the goings-on in Europe for quite some time and it didn't take long for the Allied planners to realize that the skies had become a much more dangerous place than they had been during WW I. This was especially true for those men flying the observation planes, striving to get timely and accurate information about the enemy forces to their commanders in Britain. These slow and ungainly aircraft were no match for the new breed of fighter planes that had taken to the skies and many were shot down. The Royal Air Force (*RAF*) quickly seized upon the notion of outfitting their Spitfires and Hurricanes with cameras and these new reconnaissance platforms met with great success. When the United States formally entered the war in December 1941, the United States Army Air Corp took this lesson to heart. In April of 1942, the Photographic Reconnaissance Operational Training Unit was activated at Colorado Springs (Colorado) Municipal Airport. Shortly thereafter, on June 20, 1942, the 14th Photographic Reconnaissance Squadron was one of five squadrons activated and assigned to the field.

Insignia of the 14th PRS. This drawing of Bugs Bunny flying a stylized P-38 represented the 14th from 1942 until 1975. (USAF)

The 14th joined several other units that had transferred from various locations throughout the country and drew its cadre of personnel from one of them, the newly designated 7th PRS, which one month prior had moved from Hunter Field, Savannah, Georgia. The difficulties of establishing a training base cannot be underestimated. For example, the squadron was initially headquartered in the Kaufman building on South Tejon Street in downtown Colorado Springs, miles from the field and in the middle of town. Lieutenant Colonel D. W. Hutchinson, the first Commanding Officer of what was to become Peterson Field, literally had to beg and plead for equipment and aircraft as men were pouring into his command ahead of the planes. After two months of working without airplanes or even being near a runway, the squadron was moved to the airfield.

The official history of the 14th mentions that each pilot had roughly six weeks to become what is today known as "mission ready." The syllabus consisted of getting checked out in the North American B-25 Mitchell, checking out in one of three versions of the Lockheed P-38 Lightning, and then accumulating ten or more hours in the P-38. The P-38 versions consisted of the F-4 and F-5A, which were both basically stock P-38s minus the four .50 caliber machine guns and single 20mm cannon in the nose, and the RP-322. The RP-322 was an export version of the P-38 without the turbo-superchargers normally fitted to the aircraft's engines. The pilots also spent many hours in the Link trainer, getting instrument rated in anticipation of the poor weather to be encountered overseas. Once checked out, the pilots were tasked with sorties to map the local area, mostly just for practice but occasionally "for real," meaning the results of their flights were used for commercial and military maps. Some flights were even dispatched to map sections of the Texas-Mexico border.

4 • Flying Lightning

Lt. Edward J. Peterson. (USAF /Peterson AFB Museum)

As is the case with any flying squadron, some casualties were to be expected. The first 14th pilot to die in an aircraft accident was 1st Lieutenant Edward J. Peterson. He was killed on August 8, 1942 when the F-4 he was piloting lost an engine on takeoff and crashed. The fledgling air base was renamed in his honor and Peterson Air Force Base today still shares the runways with the Colorado Springs Airport. Most pilots were a bit luckier and had about 100 hours in the F-5 and 35 hours of simulator time when the squadron was shipped out to Mount Farm, England in May, 1943. If a year seems like a long time for the squadron to get trained and ready, it is. It was a bit of administrative trickery that kept the squadron stateside for a year. In the fall of 1942, the entire squadron, which was ready for combat, was transferred to the 17th PRS and was promptly shipped overseas. This meant that the 14th had to start all over again from scratch as the pilots it received from the 17th were not yet trained.

The Engineering department, which today would be known as Maintenance, arrived at Mount Farm first and it was some time before the pilots arrived. As the 13th PRS, which had arrived some time previous, was unable to maintain its own aircraft, a contingent of 14th maintainers was temporarily assigned to the "other" squadron. According to the official squadron history, "The two-squadron maintenance system gave our mechanics an opportunity to get their first experience in maintaining aircraft for combat flying. But in a larger sense the plan failed. Our mechanics found it extremely difficult to become interested in the progress of another squadron. Also, their condemnation of the 13th's maintenance practices was open and frequent."[1]

The squadron was without aircraft until June 3, 1943 when five Supermarine Spitfire Mk. Vs were assigned to the 14th for maintenance and flying training. Again quoting from the official history, "To say that they caused confusion within the department would be a mild understatement of fact. They were the center of attraction; mechanics crawled all over them, marveling at the strange gadgets and comparing them to aircraft used by the Army Air Force. At first, there seemed to be nothing about the Spit that was in keeping with the type of aircraft we had learned to respect. The names they had for the various parts were completely baffling. Wings were no longer referred to as 'wings'; all RAF maintenance instructions called this essential part of the aircraft 'main planes'. All things considered, it was a rather tough assignment."[2] Eventually all five were put into flying shape and the mechanics who were working with the 13th were called "home" to the 14th.

One month later, on July 8, the pilots arrived. "The flight line turned into a family reunion; everybody was shaking hands, and a man who wasn't smiling was completely out of uniform. The big job was to get our pilots checked out on Spitfires, then give them plenty of local flying, which would familiarize them with the surrounding country and pave the way for combat flying. We had plenty of faith in the flying ability of these pilots, and when the time came to check them out, they didn't fail us. They all made their share of bumpy landings, of course, but when the last man had been checked out, the total damage suffered by the Spits was one broken prop. In our estimation this was a record that would top any other squadron record on the field."[3]

Only one month later, the Spitfires had to be returned and the squadron's first operational F-5As were delivered. It was quite a scramble to change planes yet again but the first F-5A was declared operational on August 12, 1943, and the squadron's first combat mission flown that same day.

Just two months later the squadron was turned upside down again as another aircraft change was made. On November 1, 1943, the definitive reconnaissance (recon) platform of the war arrived in the form of the Supermarine Spitfire Mk. XI. Both the F-5 and Spitfire were maintained and flown by the 14th for the remainder of the war and all pilots were qualified in both.

Because the 14th was the only US reconnaissance squadron flying single engine airplanes, the North American P-51 Mustang was added to the squadron roster in early 1945 to provide escort for the squadron's long range missions. Because of the late date in the war and the squadron's limited fighter experience, no kills were credited to the 14th but the pilots did claim one aircraft probably destroyed and one damaged. The squadron continued to operate all three types out of England until late 1945, when it moved to a forward location in Villacoublay, France. The squadron was disbanded immediately following the war, transferred to the Reserves and "suffered" for a brief time during the Korean War as a Troop Carrier Squadron flying C-46s. In 1953 the squadron was inactivated.

During the course of the fighting in Europe, the 14th PRS established a proud tradition, having the distinction of being the first photographic reconnaissance unit to fly single engine fighters. They received a Distinguished Unit Citation for their efforts during the spring of 1944 and seven campaign streamers. They were the first unit to fly a reconnaissance mission over the German capital of Berlin. Not surprisingly, the 14th received praise for their work in a few books written since the war. Roger Freeman, in his book *The Mighty Eighth* states:

> It was Spitfire XIs of the 14th Photo Squadron that flew most of the deep penetrations and kept watch on the important oil plants in Germany, so the Eighth Air Force was kept aware of repair activity and could decide if and when a target needed to be bombed again. Such reconnaissances were the most likely to be intercepted and the danger was not restricted to jets. On February 14th, Captain Robert Dixon took off in Spitfire PL868 for Merseburg, with three 3rd Division Mustangs escorting. On arrival it was found that Merseburg was obscured by cloud so Dixon took his Spitfire down, from 26,000 feet to about 12,000 feet before he was in the clear. Making photo runs over the Leuna works at that altitude, he was an easy target for the infamous Merseburg flak. On his fourth run the Spitfire was hit and caught fire. Dixon radioed the escort to keep clear of the area, gave them a windage correction for the homeward flight, and then described the oil plant, concluding: "Listen to this carefully. There are ten chimneys down there. Only one is smoking. This plant is almost inoperative. I'm going to bale out. Get for home at once." Successful photographic reconnaissance later backed up this description. Dixon spent the last few months of the war in a prison camp.[4]

Even the Germans acknowledged the importance of the 14th's work. A captured divisional order, issued in 1944 and quoted by Jeff Ethell and Robert Sand in their book *Fighter Command*, read in part, "Enemy aerial photo reconnaissance detects our every movement, every concentration, every weapon, and immediately after detection, every one of these objectives is smashed."[5]

The pilots of the 14th were fairly typical of other fighter pilots of the war. They started their flying training in either the PT-17 biplane or the Ryan PT-22 before moving on to the BT-13, which somewhat resembles the AT-6 Texan in appearance but has fixed landing gear and a less powerful engine. Advanced training was, however, a little different for some. Unlike most of the pure fighter guys, those destined for the reconnaissance world did not necessarily train in the North American AT-6 Texan. All of them did, however, receive some multi-engine training in a variety of aircraft. Several flights were made in the AT-9 twin engine trainer to familiarize the pilots with twin engine procedures but the majority of the time was spent in the Lockheed RP-322. Some of the pilots, including the initial cadre at Peterson Field, received training and flew practice missions in the North American B-25 Mitchell. As for the planes and missions, the squadron's 1945 yearbook describes them this way:

> In our two years of operation the squadron has flown P-38 Lightnings, the British Spitfire, and the P-51 Mustang. There were characteristics that made each suitable for a particular task.
>
> The trimetrigon camera set-up in the P-38 made it ideal for mapping. This was best illustrated on D-Day when several sweeps of P-38s covered the entire Normandy beachhead landings. The "dicing" cameras installed in the nose of some 38's were effectively used during the battle against the V-bombs when our pilots flew as low as 50 feet to photograph launching sites.

Both pilots and mechanics were glad when the easier to fly and easier to maintain "Spits" were assigned to the 14th. Their two cameras gave more exposures per roll of film and the camera's hand-ground lenses were better for recording the details of bomb damage. This, plus its higher altitude performance and longer range, is why it was used almost exclusively for Damage Assessment missions.6

Supermarine Spitfire PR Mark XI of the 14th PRS in Europe. Unlike the fighter versions, the reconnaissance Spitfires and Lightnings were painted a light blue in the hope that they would blend in with the skies at high altitude. (USAF Museum)

Arguably the prettiest airplane ever built, the Supermarine Spitfire was proof positive that "if it looks good, it will fly good." Although small in comparison to its American cousins the Mustang, Thunderbolt, and

Lightning, the Spitfire fit right in with the European design concept that produced the Hawker Hurricane and Messerschmitt Me-109. Its slender fuselage made it tough to spot in the air, but the elliptical wing planform was a dead giveaway as to its identity. The Mk. XI that the 14th flew was an improved version of the Mk. IX, which many considered to be the finest fighting Spitfire of the entire line. It improved upon its predecessors by having a more powerful engine and a four-bladed propeller to take advantage of the extra horsepower. This gave it an advertised true airspeed of 422 miles per hour (mph) at around 20,000 feet, which translates to 274 knots indicated airspeed (KIAS).

The cockpit of the Spitfire was snug, though most pilots thought this an advantage as all the controls fell easily to hand. The visibility out the canopy was as good or better than any of its contemporaries, until the Mustang came along. Even though the visibility directly to the rear was blocked, the bulged "Malcolm" hood gave the pilot the ability to lean outward and see behind.

After having the chance to sit in the cockpit of a restored Spitfire, I think that most of today's fighter pilots would get a little claustrophobic at first in the Spit. F-16 and F-15 pilots almost get the feeling that they are sitting on the aircraft rather than in it. In the Eagle, for instance, the canopy rail sits about midway between the pilot's elbows and shoulders and in the Viper the rails are just a little higher, but still below the shoulders. Sitting in the Spit, the canopy rail was just above my shoulders, and that is with the seat fully raised. The only part of my body visible from the outside was my head! The fuselage sides curve in so that my shoulders were just barely touching the sides of the cockpit. The sidewalls did curve outwards, though, so there really was plenty of room inside and I was easily able to turn around to check six. The control stick was nice and tall and the throttle quadrant was very comfortable to reach as well. The only other thing I really noticed was that the instrument panel seemed a long way away, buried under a long, curving glareshield. The overall impression I got was that the cockpit was very similar to the McDonnell Douglas A-4 Skyhawk: small and compact without being especially cramped.

Maneuverability was the strong suit of the Spitfire, no matter the model number. It had a turning capability unmatched by any fighter until the Focke-Wulf 190 came on the scene, and even that disparity was remedied with the more powerful engine of the Mk.IX.

During the course of the war, a handful of German pilots landed their aircraft at RAF bases after becoming lost or low on fuel. This gave the Allies the chance to compare their fighters directly and apply these findings to improved models. In trials against the Me-109G, the Spitfire Mk. IX was nominally faster than the Messerschmitt and could outclimb its rival, but in a dive the 109G would pull ahead. The Spitfire was, however, able to outmaneuver the 109 with ease, both in terms of roll rate and turning circle. The FW-190 was more evenly matched, having similar performance in climbs and straight away speed as well as an advantage in dives. The only advantage the Spitfire had was in turning performance, and the smart Spitfire pilot would strive to keep the fight horizontal and not get baited into a climbing and diving contest.

Like the German's Me-109, the Spitfire was designed with home defense in mind and lacked the range, speed, and *ceiling* necessary to fight the latter stages of the war over the European continent. Some changes would have to be made to turn this nimble fighter into a long range, high flying reconnaissance platform.

The RAF had seen the reconnaissance potential in the Spitfire design almost from the beginning, and the Mk.XI was simply the latest in the RAF's line of photo Spitfires. By removing the Spitfire's guns, some of the armor plate and subsequently increasing the fuel capacity, the British were able to nearly triple the Spitfire's range to over 1,300 miles. A slightly more powerful version of the Rolls-Royce Merlin developed nearly 1,700 horsepower and gave the Mk.XI a ceiling of 40,000 feet and power to spare.

Because he lacked the machine guns of the fighter plane, the reconnaissance pilot had to rely on different defensive tactics once spotted by the enemy. Normally, if an enemy is within range of his guns, the best immediate defense is a hard, maximum *G* turn into the attacker. For a reconnaissance plane, however, a tight turn might grant you a few more seconds of survival, but now you are over enemy territory, with no way to fight back, and with a couple of enemy aircraft rapidly getting back in range. The better solution is to not allow the enemy into range in the first place. The excellent high altitude and high-speed capability of the Spitfire Mk.XI made it very difficult for the Germans to attack. If the Spitfire did happen to be surprised, it still had its excellent maneuverability to fall back on plus an ability to climb out of danger.

The second plane flown by the 14th, the Lockheed P-38 Lightning, was unique in a number of ways. First of all, it was big. With a wingspan of 52 feet, the Lightning dwarfed all of its contemporaries and even a few of today's fighters! Second, its unique tricycle landing gear made for very easy taxiing and landing, and raised the aircraft high enough for pilots and maintainers to easily walk underneath the wings. Lastly, the twin engine configuration gave the Lightning a shape that was easily recognized, something which is not always a good thing in combat.

7th Photographic Reconnaissance Group (PRG) F-5, probably with the 14th PRS, at Chalgrove England, 1945. To save weight and maintenance time, the *USAAF* stopped painting most aircraft late in the war. (Keen)

Designed and put into production before the war began, the P-38 was considered by many in the European Theater as the worst of the three main US fighters in operation, the P-51 Mustang, the P-47 Thunderbolt, and the P-38. The main reason for this was that the war in Europe tended to be fought at high altitude and that was not the Lightning's preferred arena. The Pacific Theater was another story, where the majority of the top aces in theater flew the Lightning, including Richard Bong, Thomas McGuire, and Thomas Lynch. Many of the battles in the Pacific were fought at a lower altitude where the Lightning was a deadly opponent.

The cockpit was just about the right size and the bubble canopy gave excellent visibility. Similar to today's fighters, the pilot sat high in the cockpit and had plenty of room to twist and squirm in an effort to see behind. The heavy bracing, though, and the placement of the cockpit between the engines, meant the pilot had to be constantly moving his head around and turning and banking the airplane to see below the aircraft. The design of the cockpit was again unique, having a control wheel instead of the traditional stick. The wheel was well designed, though, and most pilots reported they had no problems making the transition. In fact, it actually gave the pilots an advantage at higher speeds. Because most of the fighters of the day didn't have hydraulically assisted controls (similar to power steering on a car), it took a good bit of muscle to maneuver, especially at high speed. The control wheel allowed the Lightning pilot to easily use both hands on the controls. Later models of the Lightning did have **boosted ailerons**, making things even easier.

Below 15,000 feet, the Lightning could maneuver with just about anything flying, except of course the exceptional Spitfire. The P-38 had two unique (there's that word again!) features that helped in this regard, despite its monstrous size. The first was the maneuvering flaps. By pulling back on the flap handle, conveniently located high and forward on the right cockpit sidewall, the flaps would deploy part way, increasing lift and helping to ease the control pressures. The maneuver flaps could be used at any airspeed below 250 mph. Secondly, since each propeller rotated in opposite directions, there was no torque. In most single engine fighters, the torque of the propeller pulls the nose left at high power. This also means that these fighters turn much tighter to the left than to the right. The Lightning, however, could turn equally well to the left or right, which often meant that it could turn to the right tighter than its opponent. Using a right turn as a defensive maneuver would often surprise the enemy and/or cause him to overshoot, giving the Lightning the advantage.

With two Allison engines putting out between 1,200 and 1,400 horsepower each, depending on model, the Lightning's top speed was about equal to its contemporaries. The Lightning's maximum true airspeed is in the neighborhood of 414 mph, or 269 KIAS. In fact, in the Pacific Theater, the preferred defensive maneuver was a shallow, high speed climb, maintaining about 220 KIAS to outdistance the attacker and gain enough room to turn around and make a head-on pass at the enemy.

There were, however, many traits of the P-38 that made it less than desirable at the high altitudes seen in Europe. The first was those Allison engines. For various reasons, they never worked as well at high altitude as the other fighter engines produced during the war. The P-40 Warhawk, P-39 Airacobra, and P-51A all used these same engines and all were considered obsolete or unsuitable for combat in Europe. It wasn't until the Rolls-Royce Merlin engine was fitted to the Mustang that the P-51 truly fulfilled its potential. The maximum altitude and top speed of the Lightning lagged behind the other European Theater fighters and the engines were plagued with mechanical problems as well.

Secondly, the Lightning's fairly sleek design actually worked against it in Europe. Since its top speed in level flight wasn't that great, the only way to outdistance a threat was to dive. The Lightning was one of the first of the Allied fighters to encounter a phenomenon called compressibility. At high speed the airflow over parts of the Lightning's wings would exceed the speed of sound, changing the flight characteristics of the aircraft. In the P-38, this resulted in the nose tucking under, making it difficult, if not impossible, to recover from the dive. Quite a few pilots were lost due to this before the cause was determined. As a result, severe restrictions were placed on diving the Lightning, limiting the pilot's ability to dive away from a threat or to chase after an opponent. The problem wasn't solved until late in the war with the addition of dive flaps under the wings. This problem lead to the theory of a "sound barrier" which couldn't be broken. Obviously, we know now that proper design can allow an airplane to travel faster than the speed of sound. It was these two faults, plus the easy identification afforded by its unique design, that made the Lightning somewhat of a redheaded stepchild in the skies over Europe.

14th PRS F-5 with ground crew. (Smitty Mysliwczyk/Keen)

With all of this going against it, why did the US turn the Lightning into a reconnaissance platform? The answer is range, pure and simple. At the time, the Lightning was the king of endurance and range, having a cruise range of over 1,500 miles. Without any major modifications, it could be used to fly to targets well inside the German borders. Even with its shortcomings at high altitude, it was a risk that the US felt worth taking. As you will read later, those risks could be handled with training and a bit of luck.

The third and final airplane that the 14th pilots flew was the well-known North American P-51D Mustang. The Mustang is generally considered to be the best overall piston engine fighter to see action in Europe during WW II. An argument can be made that it was the finest fighter of the entire war, though you would get some strong dissent from proponents of the marvelous Grumman F-6F Hellcat or even the Chance Vought F-4U Corsair. For all of the accolades bestowed upon the Mustang, it was an airplane that almost never was.

The Mustang wasn't even on the drawing boards when, early in 1940 the British Aircraft Purchasing Commission approached North American Aviation with a proposal for the company to produce Curtis P-40 Tomahawks under license. The president of the company, James "Dutch" Kindleberger, made a radical counter-proposal of his own; he would produce a new fighter superior to the ones the British were asking him to build! After some haggling over details, the contract was signed in May of 1940 and in the astonishing time of 117 days, North American designed and built a prototype of what would eventually become the P-51.

Fitted with the best in-line fighter engine the US could produce, the same Allison V-1710 that powered the P-38, the aircraft was delivered to the Royal Air Force. While the aircraft, named the Mustang Mk. I by the RAF and the P-51A by the US, drew rave reviews from the pilots at low altitude, it was deemed unsuitable for bomber escort or fighter sweeps over the Continent and was shipped to units dedicated to reconnaissance or ground attack. The US, which had taken delivery of the aircraft as well, came to the same conclusion but did order a dedicated ground attack version. Fitted with bomb shackles under the wings and special dive brakes on the upper wings, the plane was named the A-36 Invader and placed in service along with the P-51A. In the spring of 1942, a Rolls Royce test pilot struck upon the idea of mating his company's Merlin engine to the Mustang and the results were astounding.

The first, and to the Allied command the most important, advantage the Merlin Mustang brought to the fight was its range. The Merlin was already known as having good fuel economy, and since the Mustang could carry three times the fuel of the Spitfire Mk. V it would be an ideal bomber escort fighter, if it could fight.

7ᵗʰ PRG Mustang, squadron unknown. (Murdock/Keen)

The early Allison powered Mustangs could already maneuver at least on par with the Messerschmitts and Focke Wulfs at low altitude, and the Merlin engine gave the Mustang the ability to turn with these great fighters at all altitudes. With its new-found power, the Mustang bested the Messerschmitt in all categories except rate of climb and could outmaneuver it as well. When flown against the FW-190, though, the outcome usually depended on pilot skill as the planes were very evenly matched. Its six .50 caliber machine guns gave the Mustang a hefty punch and when combined with the amazing K-14 gunsight it was very deadly.

The K-14 was one of the first computing gunsights employed by the Allies and it also turned out to be one of the best. In order to predict how much lead was needed on a target, the sight had to know the range to the target and its direction and speed. The throttle grip on the Mustang is shaped like a motorcycle handgrip and the grip rotates just like the throttle on a motorcycle. By rotating the handgrip, the pilot changed the size of the reticle displayed on the face of the sight. Gyroscopes were installed in the gunsight itself to determine how hard the airplane was turning.

To use the sight, the pilot first had to identify the target and select the target's wingspan from a dial on the face of the sight. Lining up the target in the sight, the pilot had to then track the target for at least one second while at the same time rotating the throttle as range decreased to keep the reticle size the same size as the target. Once the target has been tracked like this for at least one second, and assuming that the target didn't change the direction it was flying, the sight would now display the proper amount of lead required for a hit. While the few pilots who were good marksmen preferred the manual sight, the vast majority of fighter pilots found the K-14 easy to use and accurate.

The bubble canopy, the single most distinctive feature of the P-51D, was a great advantage in combat because of the excellent visibility it afforded. Not introduced until the D model, the canopy caused a slight reduction in stability and top speed but the advantages far outweighed this small drop in performance. Even with the added drag of the bubble canopy, the Mustang could reach 437 mph, or 284 KIAS, making it the fastest of the planes flown by the 14th.

Like many great fighters, the Mustang demanded the most out of its pilots before it would perform at its best. In a lightly loaded configuration, the Mustang flew nicely and was very well behaved. When loaded for combat, however, and when flown to the edge of its envelope, it required a firm but at the same time delicate touch. Some will call it dangerous, but those who learned how to listen to the Mustang and heed its warnings say there isn't a sweeter plane to fly, in combat or out.

Many of these opinions were formed in the context of the day. A plane that at the time was considered stable and easy to fly might be deemed squirrelly and temperamental by a pilot flying the F-15 or F-16. To a pilot used to radar, air-to-air missiles, pressurized cockpits, and 30,000 pounds of thrust from a jet engine a comment like, "The P-51 could turn well and had a lot of power above 25,000 feet," doesn't really hold much meaning.

To further complicate matters, most pilot reports on WW II fighters are written by pilots who are not always familiar with today's fighters and the comparisons they make are usually to other WW II fighters or to civilian general aviation aircraft. To remedy this, and because I was simply dying to fly one of the worlds greatest fighters, I took the plunge and shelled out a lot of money to get some flight time in a P-51, plus the fact that my wife Joanie is a really cool chick and she said I could!

Stallion 51 Corporation, based in Kissimmee, Florida, is dedicated to promoting safety and education in the world's surviving P-51 community. They have effectively taken the lead in ensuring that the P-51 will be around and flying for many years to come. To that end, they own two beautifully restored, dual control Mustangs and they offer both checkout training and orientation flights. They offer the training to anyone willing to shell out the time and money it takes to get proficient flying the Mustang and in fact, many insurance companies require or strongly suggest that their Mustang-flying clients take this training. The orientation flights are open to anybody who wants to spend some time flying the Mustang. For me in particular, I wanted to explore the high altitude capabilities of the Mustang, get a feel for its turn performance and engine power, and investigate its slow speed flying qualities.

Since most of the war in Europe occurred at 20,000 feet and above, or at least started there before degenerating to a low altitude fight, I wanted to see for myself just what a WW II fighter felt like to fly at those altitudes. This is the same general region that fighters fly and fight in today and it just blows my mind that in the 60 years since WW II this one facet of air combat hasn't changed. As for the turn performance, I wanted to quantify what it meant to be able to "maneuver on par with" the other fighters of the day. What sort of roll rate did the Mustang have? What kind of turn rate and radius could I expect? How were the control forces compared to the F-16? How much airspeed would I lose in a break turn (maximum performance turn)? Lastly, I wanted to see what exactly the Mustang had done to earn a reputation as being dangerous when stalled.

Those who have flown her give the Mustang a great deal of respect because the consequences of a low altitude stall are typically fatal. The Mustang was particularly tricky to fly when the fuselage fuel tank was full. With the tank filled, the plane's center of gravity would shift too far to the rear, making the plane extremely tail heavy and it was very easy to lose control during any sort of maneuvering. After the war pilots were not allowed to fly with more than 65 of the tank's 85-gallon capacity filled and aerobatics were prohibited until the tank was empty.

A couple of caveats before I dive into my "evaluation." I am not a test pilot, have never claimed to be one, and probably never will be able to fly precisely enough to become one. I am a fighter pilot with a lot of experience in the F-16, a couple hours in the back seat of an F-15, one flight in the back of an F-4E, and one hour of front seat time in a F/A-18B. My time in propeller driven aircraft has been limited to single engine, fixed landing gear, non-turbocharged, fixed pitch general aviation aircraft like the Cessna 172 and Piper Warrior. My only tailwheel time is about one hour in a DeHavilland Beaver. As such, my "evaluation" is not scientific. No true evaluation of an airplane as a fighter can be made without spending many more hours in the cockpit than I had in the Mustang. A proficient pilot would no doubt be able to coax better turn performance out of the P-51, for instance, than I was able to get. Many of my conclusions are drawn from hastily scribbled notes I made during the flight or from watching the video of the flight shot through a camera mounted on the tail. To measure turn rate, for example, I said in the tape that I was going to make a 90-degree turn to the left, and after the flight I measured how long it took from starting the turn until rolling out. Hardly rocket science!

North American P-51D Mustang. (Joanie Thole)

First a little about the plane itself. Crazy Horse has probably been written about more than any other restored Mustang flying today. It is a P-51D that was modified after the war to dual control configuration, with a full set of controls and flight instruments in the back seat in place of the radio rack and the dreaded 85-gallon fuselage fuel tank found on the single seat version. With the exception of the bulletproof windscreen, it appears that all of the armor plating has been removed, along with all of the armament and associated hardware, wiring, switches, etc. I say "appears" because I didn't ask the question but it seems reasonable. Besides the stripping of armor and armament, two modifications done to Crazy Horse make it perform different than its WW II siblings. One is the replacement of the 20-pound bobweight on the elevator controls with a nine-pound version. This weight was originally added to the wartime Mustangs to make the controls heavier in pitch to counteract the tail-heavy tendencies of the fully loaded plane. The second is the larger vertical tail designed for the P-51H. What this boils down to is that I would be flying a much nicer behaving, higher performing Mustang than the 19 and 20 year olds of WW II would have enjoyed.

Offsetting this to some degree was the fact that the pilots at Stallion 51 really baby their engines. During the course of my flight, full power was never allowed and G loadings were kept to a minimum. The twelve cylinder, Packard built, Rolls Royce V 1650-7 Merlin engine is rated at 1,490 horsepower at a whopping 61 inches of manifold pressure and 3,000 revolutions per minute (rpm). For reference, most general aviation airplanes flying today have no more than 300 horsepower and the turbocharged ones reach approximately 30 inches of manifold pressure. For my flight we never went over 55 inches, not even on takeoff. Most of my maneuvering was done at a leisurely 36 inches and 2,700 rpm. While this accomplishes the goal of extending engine life, turn rate and energy bleed suffered.

Even though I have walked around countless Mustangs at airshows and in museums, I was not prepared for how big the airplane seemed now that I was actually going to fly it. With a 37-foot wingspan, the Mustang is slightly smaller overall than the F-16, but the massive 11 foot, two inch propeller and three-point stance gives the Mustang a large, aggressive look, just sitting on the ground. The top of the four-blade, Hamilton Standard propeller sits almost 14 feet off the ground, and even the spinner was just above my outstretched hand.

After a quick walk around with Eliot Cross, one of Stallion 51's pilots, I scrambled up on the left wing and into the rear cockpit. Unfortunately for me, Eliot is a very principled man and politely refused all of the bribes I offered him to allow me to sit up front! Even though I flew from the back, I did get to spend some time in the "front office" after the flight and all of my observations will be made from that perspective. Stallion 51 has heavily modified their instrument panel, adding a slew of modern instruments and grouping most of the switches on the right hand side of the panel. All of the hardware though, such as the trim wheels, flaps, etc., are all still in the standard location. Because of this, I will reference the stock Mustang configuration for my comments.

The cockpit is snug, without being uncomfortable. Not as tight as the Spitfire, but nowhere near as roomy as an Eagle. Very Viper sized, I would say. The throttle quadrant is located on the left sidewall, a little higher than I am used to but not uncomfortably so. With your hand wrapped around the throttle grip, it is very easy to maneuver the prop control lever with your thumb and your hand has to come off of the throttle and slightly aft to change the mixture. The trim wheels are very conveniently located along the left sidewall as well, below the throttle quadrant and also slightly aft. The only lever difficult to get to was the flaps. The flap handle is next to the seat, located down by your left hip. This might have proved difficult to reach while wearing bulky winter flying gear and probably took some practice for a pilot to get comfortable using in combat. The landing gear lever is low and forward, next to the pilot's left knee. The levers to jettison the bombs/external fuel tanks are nicely placed between the throttle and landing gear lever and slightly forward.

By today's standards the instrument panel is a bit of a mess. The flight instruments are mostly to the center and the left, and the engine instruments are mostly on the right. In fairness, the design is probably as good as any other WW II fighter but great strides have been made since then. The actual arrangement of the dials is different, but I would say flying instruments in the P-51 would be a lot like flying instruments in the T-37, for those of you with time in that fine machine. In the weather, you will be constantly moving your eyes and head all over the place in order to view the pertinent instruments. The lower portion of the panel and the center console is devoted to armament switches, engine control switches such as the magnetos, starter, and supercharger controls, and the fuel tank selector. The right sidewall of the cockpit houses the majority of the electrical switches and the radios. All in all, it is well designed for combat and I don't think it would take long at all to feel comfortable.

Engine start and taxi were what you would expect, with two exceptions. One was the absolute lack of forward visibility. Common in all tail-wheel airplanes, this trait is magnified in the Mustang by the ten feet or so of cowling that seems to stretch forever in front of you. Taxiing requires a constant S-turn and you have to stick your head out in the windstream as you do so to see ahead. Taxiing in the rain would not be any fun! But, it was easy to get the hang of and the Mustang handles very well on the ground. With the stick aft of neutral, the tail wheel is steerable via the rudder pedals and with the stick forward, it swivels freely to allow for close-in maneuvering.

"Crazy Horse" taxis for takeoff at Kissimmee airport. (Joanie Thole)

Second, almost every pilot report written on the Mustang says that the engine noise is something else. I am here to tell you, it was LOUD! Even wearing earplugs underneath my flying helmet, I was totally unprepared for the wall of noise rushing back from the twelve exhaust stacks just feet in front of the cockpit. When we taxied to the end of the runway, we had to wait a minute and a half for the engine oil temperature to rise within limits before we could do the pre-takeoff engine checks. When Eliot ran the power up to 2300 rpm, there was no doubt that this was a powerful beast. The airplane was buffeting and shaking, just dying to get airborne. Closing the canopy really didn't help much either. How any WW II fighter pilots have any hearing left I'll never know.

It was now time to get airborne and turn this noise into airspeed and altitude. Eliot, once again the man of steel nerves and unshakeable ethics, refused my bribes yet again and did the takeoff himself. At our weight, the book says the Mustang will reach its minimum liftoff speed of about 90 KIAS in around 1000 feet. This is surprisingly similar to the acceleration of a **mil power** takeoff in a Block 42 F-16. It also warns, "Do not jam the throttle forward, as torque will cause loss of control of the airplane."[7] Even with the recommended 6 degrees of right rudder trim set for takeoff, Eliot waited until the tail was off the ground before setting 55 inches manifold pressure. Soon after raising the gear, we pulled the power back to 46 inches. Once out of traffic and headed on course, Eliot handed the plane off to me and with the exception of one touch and go I did the remainder of the flying.

Finally airborne, I was very pleasantly surprised with the visibility in flight. Even with my helmet on, I had plenty of room to twist and turn around in the cockpit without bashing my noggin on the canopy. It was very easy to see behind, though in the combat models the armor-plated headrest would restrict your visibility directly to the rear. The canopy rails sit just below shoulder level, affording an excellent view to the sides. As for the view forward, surprise was again the word. Eliot's helmet is exactly the same shade of blue as the cowling so I hardly noticed him sitting directly in front of me. The only time in flight that the nose of the airplane would be a factor would be at low level, as it would block the view of the terrain for a few miles in front of the aircraft.

Forty six inches and 2,700 rpm is the maximum continuous power setting and this gave us a climb rate of between 1,500 and 2,000 feet per minute at 150 knots. The book says that a combat-loaded (two 75-gallon wing tanks) Mustang would give you a climb rate of 1,200 feet per minute to 20,000 feet at that power setting. We climbed directly to 16,000 feet; 18,000 feet is the highest we saw during the flight. I wanted to sample the turn performance above 20,000 feet, but that would have required an Instrument Flight Rules (IFR) clearance which would have been too much of a hassle for this sortie. The engine was still barely able to give me 46 inches at full throttle as we leveled out.

I got my first lesson in engine management as we climbed. The Mustang is one of the first US fighters to try to simplify the pilot's job of managing the engine, with the mixture, manifold pressure, supercharger, and oil and radiator coolant doors all having automatic settings. The mixture control, for example, only has three settings: IDLE CUTOFF, NORMAL, and RICH. I would think that during an average combat sortie, the pilot would have to spend minimal time messing with the throttle or supercharger to keep the engine in limits. Since this was not a combat sortie, however, I had to do a little more work. The manifold pressure regulator only works between 42 and 61 inches, and since we spent most of our time below that Eliot was very mindful of the manifold pressure gauge as I flailed about the sky. Secondly, the two-speed supercharger is programmed to switch automatically to high blower between 15,700 and 19,700 feet. Again, since we were below this most of the day, we manually placed the supercharger control in LOW BLOWER for the entire flight, except for our speed run. I was therefore surprised to have to continually adjust the throttle to maintain a constant power setting as we climbed and dived. The RPM stayed put all day.

The first item on the agenda was the speed run. Switching to high blower, I thumbed the prop lever full forward to 3,000 rpm, and advanced the throttle to 55 inches (our self imposed limit) to see what she would do. Not surprisingly, the acceleration at altitude was not brisk. After quite some time, Crazy Horse settled down at 250 KIAS at 16,000 feet. For some reason I expected more out of the airplane, but I shouldn't have, given the advertised maximum airspeed of 284 KIAS. In retrospect, this was just about right on since we weren't at full power and we also lost a few knots because the canopy fitted to Crazy Horse is slightly bigger than that on a stock –D model. All in all, highly respectable performance for a propeller driven airplane.

To put this in perspective for all you fighter pilots and wannabes out there, the corner velocity (airspeed which will produce the quickest, tightest turn) of the Mustang is around 225 KIAS at an astounding eight Gs. Not surprising, then, that many of the fighter pilots in both theaters made it a rule not to go below this airspeed if at all possible. You wouldn't really want to cruise around much faster than this either, as in doing so you are actually going too fast to make your best defensive turn. Plus, you'd be using a lot of gas.

As far as the overall flying qualities of the airplane, the P-51 flew nothing like I had expected. It wasn't good or bad, just completely different. For example, when the airplane was new many reports said the Mustang was unstable in cruise flight and could not be trimmed to fly "hands off". They made this sound like a bad thing. I found the Mustang to be fine in cruise flight, and the slight deviations in flight path when I released the controls to take notes did not seem excessive. My opinion might change if I had to fly eight-hour sorties four times a week without an autopilot! The trim controls were very effective, with just slight movement of the trim wheel necessary with large changes in airspeed. The rudder was very easy to coordinate with the ailerons, and I had the impression of just using pressure on the rudder pedals during turns as opposed to actually moving them. My tendency during the entire flight was to use way too much rudder.

The control forces in pitch and roll were heavier than I had expected and the roll rate was slower than anticipated. After three attempts, the best roll rate I could produce was 90 degrees per second at 210 KIAS. Eliot said I could probably get 120 or so from the front cockpit with practice.

The rear cockpit is narrower and your leg gets in the way of the stick when rolling. This roll rate is less than a fully loaded F-16 so I was indeed surprised. In pitch, the Mustang was responsive but again the control forces were higher than I expected. When maneuvering at high speed I can imagine you would be doing a lot of two-handed pulling. The best turn rate I could get was in the neighborhood of 14 degrees per second. I'm sure the plane will do better than this as we were only using 36 inches of power and 210 knots. At that power setting we quickly reached the buffet preceding the stall. The eight G load limit at 225 KIAS promises very tight turns. Overall, much like the real thing, this Mustang gave me the impression that she will go where you tell her. You just have to be forceful about it!

As for the slow speed handling, I got exactly what I expected. There is very little buffet until just prior to the stall, making for an excellent gun platform. The ailerons get a little mushy approaching the stall, but so do every other airplane's. About ten knots prior to the stall, you get a decent buffet in the seat of the pants and through the stick, and then she breaks. We did our straight-ahead stalls at 24 inches and 3,000 rpm. Both times the right wing dropped abruptly to 45 degrees and the nose fell. Recovery was rapid with a release of the stick. Because of my limited experience in the P-51 and the Mustang's notorious behavior at high power and low airspeed, Eliot had me make the recoveries without adding power. Even so, the airplane got back to flying as soon as I quit pulling on the stick.

We then did a couple of accelerated stalls. I left the power at 24 inches and 3,000 rpm, slowed to about 130 KIAS, and rolled into a 60-degree turn to the left. Again, the Mustang turned smoothly and predictably and I had no trouble anticipating the stall due to the buffet. The stall itself knocked my socks off! After less than one second of buffet, the Mustang bucked 90 degrees to the left, putting us into 135-degrees of bank! We did it once more with the same result. Both times, hard right stick and rudder along with a release of the back pressure brought us right out. I can't even imagine what kind of ride we would have had at full throttle or if I had kept pulling!

Given my experience, I thought the stall was rather abrupt but with good warning. The flight manual nonchalantly states, "The airplane has a comparatively mild stall. The airplane doesn't whip at the stall, but rolls rather slowly and has very little tendency to drop into a spin."[8] Again, I guess it all depends on what you are comparing it to!

Aerobatics was the last item on the list before heading back. I pretty much held 36 inches and 2,700 rpm throughout, with Eliot keeping careful eye on the manifold pressure gauge since we were below the 42 inches necessary for the regulator to take charge. The plane had plenty of power to spare and I did a couple loops, a half Cuban-eight, one Immelman, and two cloverleafs. All were done with around 260 to 280 KIAS, although in combat the plane would certainly loop at less using full power. I again noticed that the stick forces were higher than expected, the roll rate slower, and I overcorrected on the rudder every time I tried to roll, especially at the top of the Immelman as I sent the nose of the airplane slicing to the side as we rolled out! About this time Eliot got tired of me making a mockery of his airplane and we headed back to the field.

We made our descent from 15,000 feet with the power pulled back to 26 inches and 2,400 rpm. Even at that, the Mustang showed its true colors as it picked up speed in a heartbeat and Eliot had to scold me into reducing our airspeed from the 300 KIAS I had been carrying so as to stay legal with the FAA. Leveling off at 2,000 feet, the Mustang gave a smooth ride even with the gusty winds and cumulous clouds in the area. About three miles from the field, Eliot took the plane and demonstrated a touch and go for me, promising me I'd get to do the next one to a full stop.

Now, I've spent many hours as a student in various different airplanes, and if Eliot was manipulating the controls or trim wheels when I was flying I couldn't tell. Because of this and because it makes me feel important, I will continue to believe that I actually did land the Mustang and will write about it as such! Eliot handed me the controls on downwind at about 150 KIAS. There were a couple of other planes in the pattern so we flew a standard rectangular pattern, extending our downwind to have enough room behind the traffic. At the base turn, power came back to around 23 inches and pretty much stayed there. Flaps came down to full turning final and the Mustang settled down to 110 KIAS. Visibility on final was excellent and I forgot that I was sitting in the back. Trim changes were minimal and it was easy to counteract the ten-knot crosswind with a slight crab to the right. As we flared to touchdown, I fed in a little left rudder to align with the runway and a little right stick to stop the drift. I was happy with my approximation of a wheel landing and I kept the stick coming back to put the tailwheel on the ground. That's when the fun started. As the tail came down, that big nose came up and suddenly all I could see in front of me was blue cowling and the Mustang started trying to leave the runway! Anybody who has landed a tailwheel airplane knows that the real work starts when the tail hits the ground. Luckily, the runway was wide, giving me plenty of cues out the sides of the canopy as to how poor a job I was doing of going straight! The Mustang is actually much tamer than most due to the steerable tailwheel and with some encouragement from Eliot I was able to keep the beast on the runway and rolling out in a semi-straight line. I think that as long as a new Mustang pilot avoided stalling the airplane in the pattern and respected all of the power in that Merlin engine he would have no trouble at all learning how to land it.

Overall, it was a very eye opening and thoroughly enjoyable experience. I had expected a nimbler airplane but I was in no way disappointed. I walked away with a much deeper understanding of what it must have been like fighting in the Mustang. I have nothing but good things to say about Stallion 51 and Eliot Cross, who came in on a holiday to shepherd this Mustang pilot wannabe around for a few hours. The biggest compliment I can give him is that even though I knew he had done this hundreds of times, I felt like I was the one and only customer he has ever taken up on an orientation ride. He displayed nothing but professionalism and enthusiasm for what he does and a willingness to share it with others.

Bruce Fish

Bruce Fish is typical of the pilots in the 14th. He graduated pilot training in 1943 from Williams Field, Arizona, and went to follow-on training at Will Rogers Field in Oklahoma. I asked him to tell about the aircraft he flew and their strong and weak points. I also asked about the types of reconnaissance he did. Was it all done taking pictures or was there a bit of the old, "look out the window and take notes on what you see"? Lastly, I was curious about the tactics he used to avoid and/or defeat any threats, be they from flak (now referred to as Anti-aircraft Artillery or "triple A") or from enemy fighters. He recalls:

> I was in Class 43I, starting Primary training in PT-17s at Thunderbird, Phoenix, Arizona. Basic training was flown in BT-13s at Pecos, Texas and Advanced training in the AT-9, AT-6, and P-38 at Williams Field, Arizona. Flying time in the AT-6 was evenly split between instruments, formation, and gunnery with about 8 hours each. I flew 17 hours of twin-engine practice in the AT-9 and 15 hours in the P-38 or RP-322. Fighter training at Will Rogers Field in Oklahoma got me to England with 80 hours in P-38s, 34 hours in the Link simulator, and maybe ten hours of instrument time in UC-78s and B-25s.
>
> Looking back, we should have been locked up if there was even a high cirrus cloud layer at 30,000 feet, but here we were in "Jolly Old England" about to learn instrument flying in a hurry, the hard way! Navigation facilities were nil, except for a direction finding station that was not very accurate and had very limited range.
>
> I was assigned to the 7th Photo Group, 325th Photo Wing. The 7th had three squadrons of P-38s and one squadron of Spitfires and P-38s, the 14th. Luckily, I was assigned to the 14th. I flew the F-5 on missions about a

third of the time. In the meantime, we got to fly five hours in a Spitfire Mk. VB and another couple of hours in the Spitfire Mk. XI before starting operations in both the F-5 and Spitfire.

The Spitfire, combat wise, was superior to the F-5 or I probably wouldn't be here. It had a slight edge in straight and level speed at all altitudes, a big advantage in rate of climb at all altitudes, and at least a 10,000-foot combat ceiling advantage. A typical mission profile from England, flying 400 to 500 miles into Europe, was to *cruise climb* to 40,000 feet, drop to 30,000 feet at the target area, photo targets, and cruise home at 30,000 to 40,000 feet. You just had to keep your eyes open and easily evade any German surprises.

I think most Spit losses were pilot error, mechanical problems or weather. The F-5, without the finesse of the Spit, had these same problems plus it flew in the same flight levels as the Germans without having any distinct advantages. The Germans also knew that the Mustang had replaced the P-38 type fighters, so any P-38 types were flying recon with no guns. Low-level missions were flown in the P-38 with *oblique cameras.* Of course more visual recon was obtained at low-level and losses were higher! There were also P-51 squadrons doing this low-level work. They did the visual recon and we did the strategic photo work. You can't see much detail at 30,000 feet.

In late 1944 the 14th was given P-51Ds to be used to escort the real long-range missions of both the Spits and Lightnings of all 7th Photo Reconnaissance Group (PRG) aircraft. The 14th got the job because of single engine experience and because a few of us had fighter training. All 14th pilots trained for and flew this mission. We would escort the P-38s with a flight of four P-51s on special missions three to four times per week. This tactic was devised because of the increased activity of the ME-262 that got more than a few of our Lightnings. Sorry to say it wasn't reciprocal. It was too small an effort to do much good except to give the photo plane a head start. Soon all P-38 squadrons had their own P-51s. They received training or were sent fully trained fighter pilots.

We didn't really need escort with the Spitfires. I felt safer alone! We got to 30,000 feet twice as fast as the 51 could with tanks (external fuel tanks) so we would waste fuel and time circling the 51 on climb out. The 51s provided more eyes to clear our area but they also made us easier to see. The Spit was better off alone, with a climbing turn no other aircraft could stay with, except for the jet and rocket powered ones.

The Spitfire is my all time favorite aircraft from a pilot's standpoint. Like trying to fly a butterfly. Had to be on top of that lady every second.

Dave Thole • 35

14th PRS Spitfire Mk. XI. (USAF Museum)

The Lightning was the best photo platform as the cameras could be interchanged from 6, 12, 24, 36, and 40- inch focal plane and placed in all vertical and oblique positions. The Spit had two vertical 40- inch cameras placed behind the pilot, period. They developed an RF-51 with a recon package for the 9th Air Force with a system similar to the Spit. I flew combat in them in Korea with the 45th Tactical Reconnaissance Squadron (TRS). They were the guys that mostly looked out the window.

We all saw lots of German aircraft but did our best to keep them at a distance. Our job was to get to the target, take our pictures, and get them back for intelligence. The 7th PRG did that job well!9

James Fellwock

James G. "Jim" Fellwock, Lt Col, USAF (Retired) was another pilot with the 14th and was kind enough to let me reprint some of his memoirs that he wrote in 1992 for his grandchildren. His training was similar to Bruce Fish's and we pick up his story shortly after he arrived in England.

On August 27, 1944, I was checked out in an old Spitfire Mk. V, one that had actually been used in the Battle of Britain. It was powered by a superb Rolls Royce Merlin engine, the horsepower of which I cannot recall, but it was plenty. Flying became fun again! This little plane had speed, maneuverability, and handled like a dream. It was receptive to every minute instruction it was given and literally jumped in response. Landing was a bit tricky at first, having gotten used to the tricycle landing gear of the P-38. Once the landing was made in a 38 it rolled down the runway as straight as an arrow. Not so the Spit. You had to stay right on top of the rudders and brakes until you came to a full stop. There were many *groundloops* at first by many of the newly checked out, but as experience was gained it was not too much different than the AT-6 once you got used to it.

Fortunately I had no problems with the Spit. Like my Betty and I, I think the Spitfire and I were made for each other. The first few times up in that wonderful little plane, particularly the Mk. V, was, indeed, love at first flight. You cannot believe just how much pure enjoyment can be derived from putting the Spitfire through its maneuvers. After flying the P-38 it was really a joy. The P-38 was big, fast, solid, heavy, and hard to fly. By "hard" I don't mean difficult, I mean **hard**. It took muscle to put a 38 through its maneuvers. Later versions of the F-5 and P-38 had boosted ailerons and that was a great help but it was still a far cry from the Spit. I flew that wonderful little airplane, the Mk. V, four times before graduating into the much newer and fully operational Spitfire Mk. XI.

The Mk. XI, much like the operational F-5, had been stripped of its guns, of course, and all armor plating to reduce overall weight. When in combat the evasive action for an F-5 when attacked was to put its nose down slightly, the throttle through the firewall, and fly away from the enemy. By pressing the throttle slightly to the right it was possible to increase power just a bit more. This was marked "War Emergency" and was referred to by most of us as "through the firewall". In the Spitfire it was "through the firewall" and stand that little plane on its tail and climb away from the enemy. I only had to use these procedures a few times but I am here today to say that they worked for me, and many others I'm sure.

D-Day, of course, was June 6th, 1944. Every Allied aircraft from the smallest to the largest was still sporting invasion stripes under each wing when I arrived at Mt. Farm. My first mission was in an F-5 to photograph bomb damage in an area of France just south of Brest. The first mission for each new replacement was always a very short, no risk jaunt over and back so that each man could have his picture taken with the Squadron Commanding Officer (CO) for a write up in the local newspaper back home. My first was no different. I did look a little odd, however, without a pair of goggles on my helmet. There was really no need for goggles as the canopy was closed tight from takeoff to landing and the only reason we wore the helmet at all was for the built in radio earphones and warmth. Our CO at the time was a very nice guy by the name of Capt. Robert J. Dixon. Unfortunately, he too just didn't return from a mission one day. Well, so much for mission Number One. The big press release did make the Riverside Press Enterprise and I was on my way toward the big 50-mission mark.

D-Day really marked the beginning of the end for Adolf Hitler but he wasn't to go down easily. The combined Air Forces of Great Britain and the United States pounded German aircraft plants and all manufacturing plants that made anything for their war effort. When these were pretty well destroyed we went after her oil refineries in an effort to cut off the life-blood of her war machines. Considering this, the main objective of Photo Recon at this time was Bomb Damage Assessment.

A typical day would find us photo recon pilots walking down to breakfast before checking in at Operations (Ops). As we walked the B-17s would be forming up overhead getting ready for their daily missions. After we ate we would go to Ops and check the board. Each pilot had a cardboard tag with his name on it and it was hung one above the other on a tall board. As the top pilots were assigned missions the tags were all moved up. If your turn was today you would be assigned a target and usually an alternate just in case. We then would check the weather, sit down, and start plotting out our maps. In Photo Recon, one target was covered by one airplane with one pilot. Once you took off on a mission there was no contact with anyone until you were back over the field ready to come in and land. With the maps all made out and all of our heavy gear on we would pile on a Jeep and someone would drive us to the line. There the F-5 or Spitfire was all gassed, cameras loaded, engines warmed up and ready to go. Within a few minutes I was in the air. As the war progressed the targets became farther and farther away, consequently it would take longer and longer to get to them. This also made it necessary to carry drop tanks to get there and back. The routine of the mission was the same either way. Usually, shortly before I would arrive at the target, I would meet the B-17s on their way back home after having dropped their bombs. We usually flew at around 30,000 feet, sometimes higher and sometimes lower, but that would keep us well above the B-17s and high enough to get a good look at how they did. After I photographed the entire area I would start home and somewhere along the way pass the B-17s again. When we reached the English Channel we were almost home so we could start to let down a bit. Let down in altitude, that is, and relax a bit too. Once back at the field and on the ground we would go back to Ops for interrogation to tell them just what we thought we had seen and photographed. This completed, we would head back to our Nissen hut home to sack out. Somewhere along that walk we could hear, and watch sometimes, the B-17s coming back from their missions.

Very shortly after I got to Mt. Farm and got settled in Bob Hilburn, the young 2nd Lieutenant who gave Betty away at our wedding, didn't return from a mission. It couldn't have been more than his third or fourth mission. He just didn't come back from the mission he had been assigned.

September the 8th, 1944, stands out vividly in my memory. Up until this time the Germans had been using V-1 Buzz Bombs to bomb London. This was an unmanned, jet powered, flying bomb. It was fast, but catchable by English fighter planes. They sent so many over, however, it was impossible to knock them all down. Ground fire from anti-aircraft guns did as well as anything. Oddly enough, they would sound in flight much like a washing machine, chug-chugging along. If you were nearby and heard one of them in the vicinity you were all right as long as you could hear it chugging. As soon as the engine stopped, however, hit the deck! It was coming down somewhere. Unfortunately, Adolf had more tricks up his sleeve and as it happened I was right there to see the first of them.

It was called the V-2 and for all intents and purposes was the forerunner of today's Inter-Continental Ballistic Missile, the ICBM. I was enroute to a target somewhere in Germany when off my left wing I noticed a contrail starting from the ground and going straight up. It kept climbing straight up until it reached my altitude. I was flying between 25,000 and 30,000 feet. Once that high it continued to what I estimated was at least 50,000 feet. We could fly a supercharged 38 or Spit to about 40,000 or 41,000 feet but up in that thin air it was just barely hanging there like on a thread. This thing was well above that. As it climbed the last few thousand feet it started to bend over toward England and ultimately, I was to understand later, to London. When the mission was over and each of the photo planes that were out that day were back at Ops it sounded like a beehive of activity. It seems that we had witnessed the first launch of a V-2 from Germany. Evidently Allied Intelligence knew about it beforehand but did not know just when it would be launched. History has recorded that this was the first of many V-2s that did a tremendous amount of damage to an already badly bombed London. In spite of this and through it all, they did survive.

About this time General Patton's troops were surging forward toward Germany herself and he wanted up to date photo maps of the country-side ahead of him. The whole area was socked in with cloud cover so that was impossible. It was under cover of this bad weather that the Germans launched the Battle of the Bulge in December of 1944. December 24th, Christmas Eve, I flew a C-47 over to the front loaded with the latest reconnaissance photos and Christmas day was just like any other day. I don't remember how many missions were flown out of Mt. Farm that day but I was one of them. We had all been going somewhere most every day. My target this day was a bridge in Belgium near where the battle was taking place. Our field was completely socked in with a ceiling of zero so takeoff was all instruments from the time the wheels came up. Just my cup of (bitter) tea. Oh, how good it felt to pop through the top of those clouds into the bright sunlight. The weather over the target area was supposed to be partly cloudy but I think there were a lot of crossed fingers when they made that forecast. When I reached the approximate area of the target there was nothing to be seen in any direction but clouds, except, and I couldn't believe my eyes, one hole and at the bottom of that hole was a river and a bridge. I couldn't rack that little Spit around fast enough but I was able to get a picture of that bridge. I felt as if I had single-handedly won the war in doing so! After flying back and forth several more times just in case another hole would open up I finally started back to base. Once back over England it was quite evident that Mt. Farm was still socked in so I was told to use a Royal Air Force base in northern England that was open. This I did with no problem. The thing that still sticks in my mind about that whole mission was the Christmas dinner at that English air base. No meat, brussel sprouts, and I believe hard English white cheese. It humbles a person somewhat to realize just how rough the English had it during the war. We lived like kings by comparison. Oh yes, I did fly back to Mt. Farm the next day as the weather had finally broken. My film was quickly processed and when the pictures were printed my balloon was promptly burst. I was told that I had great pictures of a bridge, all right, but it was not the right one.

The first part of 1945 saw the massive air assaults by the British Sterling and Halifax bombers at night and the B-17s and B-24s during the day on German oil. There were many days flying over Germany when there wasn't a cloud to be seen but the whole sky below was almost covered with contrails from the many airplanes in the sky. The devastation must have been overwhelming.

Sometime during the first part of 1945 the Germans started using yet another new weapon. This time it was rocket and jet aircraft. Though still in experimental stages they did shoot down many Allied airplanes. One small, light blue airplane, either P-38 or Spitfire, flying at high altitude, would quite obviously be an unarmed Photo Recon ship. It became good sport for them to go up and pick one of us off. Some of the deeper missions into Germany would ask for, and receive, P-51 fighter escorts from the 8th Air Force (AF). It soon came down to the fact that 8th AF had plenty of nice new P-51Ds but no pilots to fly them. The answer was very apparent. Give the 7th Photo Group some of those nice, brand-new P-51Ds and let them fly their own fighter cover. This was all well and good but there was one small detail that was overlooked.

One small detail that if the Germans had known they could have had a field day when we showed up. Not one Photo Recon pilot, myself included, had ever had even one minute's time in or at a gunnery school! We didn't even know what it felt like to fire six .50 caliber machine guns from a moving airplane. The easy answer to this situation was to have each of us newly checked out P-51 fighter pilots take the plane out somewhere and find out first-hand just what it feels like.

There was an old derelict sunken barge just off the East Coast that someone had gotten permission for us to go and shoot at. Quite frankly, I could hardly wait to go give it a try. I found it easily and after a couple of practice runs I switched the gun switches to "on". As I dove the Mustang toward the barge I gave it a good long burst. It was fun! Every fifth or sixth shell in the outside gun belts was a tracer so you could see just where each burst was going. It was very easy to adjust if you were high or low, left or right. Clobbering that old, already clobbered barge was a real piece of cake.

After almost shooting the thing clear out of the water I decided that I had accomplished this mission and did indeed know what it felt like to fire six .50 caliber machine guns from a P-51. As I was climbing back out to return to base, however, one of the inboard guns fired one single shell. I quickly checked the gun switches and they were both off. My finger was nowhere near the trigger but at that moment, another gun went off. Malfunction was my first thought so in order not to shoot up the base with any more unfired shells I returned to the barge and made sure all six guns were empty. When I got back to Mt. Farm, I taxied up to the ramp and stopped. Each time you do this and shut down the engine the Crew Chief was up on the left wing and the Armament Chief was up on the other wing. I explained in detail the malfunction that had taken place with the gun switches and he said he would look into it for me. With that, I piled into a jeep and went back to Ops.

Later that day, the Armament Chief asked me how long the bursts were when I was shooting at the barge. I said, "Oh, I suppose around 10 to 15 seconds each." He grinned and much to my chagrin and embarrassment he informed me that I had burnt out four of the six barrels by holding down the trigger much too long! One to three second bursts were highly recommended and longer only if absolutely necessary. Thus another page in my book of learning the hard way. No one had ever told me how long to hold the trigger down.

7th PRG Mustangs somewhere in Europe. This photo was taken from the oblique camera of an F-5. (Keen)

Once I became a genuine, bona-fide Fighter Pilot, the remainder of the missions I flew were as fighter cover for our own photo planes. Most of the time it was one Photo Recon Spit or F-5, with me and a wingman on one side and another pair of Mustangs on the other side. Four fighters proved more and more to be too much for the enemy to even bother with. Our repeated B-17 bombing raids on their oil supplies and refineries were starting to pay off too. They just didn't think it was worth the fuel and effort to come up after us.

The Germans were always trying something new. I can remember one time fairly late in the war when we were feeling kind of smug up at about 30,000 feet on our way to a target when we noticed a flight of six Focke Wulf-190s quite a bit lower than we were and well behind. Just as we spotted them, they started pouring out white smoke from their engines and started more alarmingly to gain altitude and close the distance between us. There wasn't honestly much we could do other than watch. We were going as fast as we could. Fortunately after what seemed like at least half an hour the white smoke stopped and all six of them gave up the chase. We figured out later that they must have been trying out some new water injection system to increase horsepower. From where we watched it worked. It was just a good thing it worked for such a short time.

There were a few missions over Europe at very high altitude that were absolutely breathtaking. If the weather was good, the atmosphere clear, and you were flying above Belgium, then you could see Holland, Germany, Denmark, the North Sea, the bottom of Sweden, the snow covered Alps, Switzerland, Northern Italy, France and of course directly behind you England, Scotland, Wales, and a bit further west Ireland. It was almost like looking down at a map of Europe in the family atlas. I only had an opportunity to see that beautiful sight a couple of times but for those I am very grateful. Considering today's smog all over the world, I'm sure that sight is a thing of the past.[10]

John Blyth

The late Jeff Ethell, along with Robert Sand, put together an outstanding book titled *Fighter Command: Original WW II Color*. It is filled with color photographs and first hand accounts of what it was like to fly in Europe during WW II. More importantly, it also has some nice color photographs of 14th aircraft in Europe. I highly recommend it and its companion *WW II Pacific War Eagles*. Both books can be purchased through Classic Motorbooks (1-800-826-6600). John Blyth, a pilot with the 14th, recalls some of his experiences in the book.

> When I heard that we were getting enough Spitfires to equip one squadron, I asked to be transferred. I had dreamed since high school of flying a Spitfire and now it was becoming a reality. My first mission in the Spitfire Mark XI was in April 1944. I went in at 36,000 feet and was thrilled by the Spit's performance. It exceeded my expectations because it was so much more than the Mark V I had flown locally. The 1,650 hp Rolls-Royce Merlin really made a difference. I loved its response at altitude and didn't mind that it only had one engine.

Another 14th Spitfire in Europe. (USAF Museum)

I don't know about other pilots, but to me the English Channel was like an invisible wall. At some point one passed from being relatively safe to entering the unknown. Mentally, each of us probably handled it differently, but flying alone and unarmed was quite different than flying with others. Actually, I was usually busy climbing on course and navigating while crossing the Channel and tried not to think about it. Oftentimes part of the mission would be on instruments, making navigation more difficult. We often had several targets to photograph, making at least three runs over each, all the while watching for German fighters or our own fighters that figured a Spitfire in this deep must have been captured.

On the way home, it was almost guaranteed that we would face a headwind. Sometimes it seemed forever to reach the English Channel. If I was low on fuel, I would land at RAF Bradwell Bay or RAF Manston stations to refuel and make a bathroom stop. A cramped cockpit at -50 degrees is not the most comfortable work place. At altitude, the heater in the Spitfire or F-5 wasn't much good.[11]

One mission in particular sticks out in his mind.

> We refueled at RAF Manston for maximum fuel. I was at 30,000 feet on the way in and could hear the German radar pick me up. I could hear it build up and fade on my headset. Near Dresden I saw a factory that had been bombed and figured I would make a pass across it and save someone a trip. It probably saved my life! As I rolled into a turn to align the target and turned on my cameras, I noticed an aircraft diving and closing rapidly on my tail. He must have been above me and I missed him. At first I thought it was a jet because of the black exhaust trail. It was an Me-109 with a yellow prop spinner and yellow and orange checkered nose. There might have been others. In a Spit, the throttle was full forward at altitude so I pushed full forward on the propeller control to pick up speed. I flew straight and level and played like I didn't see him. He probably figured he had another victory for the Fatherland and was about to squeeze the trigger when I pulled back abruptly on the stick. Then and there we must have parted company. When I rolled into a turn and looked down, he was underneath me. The climb at that altitude surprised me. Any other evasive maneuver and he probably would have nailed me. I then remembered my cameras and turned them off.[12]

Gerald Adams

Aside from that lucky Me-109, few of the German's conventional fighters could routinely fly high enough and fast enough to intercept the Spitfires and Lightnings of the 14th. The same could not be said of the jet powered Me-262 and rocket powered Me-163. Gerald M. Adams had one of the squadron's first encounters with the Me-163. He was a lieutenant when the incident occurred, but he went on to command the 14th before war's end and retired as a Colonel. He wrote an article for the "Friends Journal," a publication available to members of the USAF Museum Foundation.

>Lousy weather over the continent that day kept the bomber and fighter planes in England. Someone in the head shed at 8th Air Force must have said, "Let's send a *reccie* plane over to see what's going on." So yours truly takes off in an F-5 to photograph seven targets in the Merseberg-Leipzig area, if possible. This reccie mission was about number 20 of a total of 55 flown in F-5 and Mk. XI Spitfire aircraft during a two year tour in the 8th Air Force.
>
>Middle and low clouds covered the continent from the English Channel well into Germany. After flying for more than an hour and a half, a break in the clouds showed two of the assigned targets. This reccie (pronounced "Wrecky") pilot had lucked out. Photo runs were made at 33,000 feet. While making a run on the second target, an aircraft appeared some distance to the east, a "bandit" German, but too far away to catch an F-5.
>
>With the second target covered and cameras turned off, another check showed the bandit uncomfortably close. Now things were getting serious. With throttles full forward

and a heading for home, another look for the bandit found him blasting away from the rear with two 30mm cannon.

The higher speed of this airplane along with the rapid puffs of exhaust smoke coming from the tail and the cannon fire coming from the nose sparked a strong desire to get the hell out of there. Down went the nose of the F-5 toward the lower clouds. The F-5 could do 400 mph straight and level, on a good day.

Clouds at 12,000 feet provided a brief sanctuary, but hauling that plane out of a vertical dive with the instrument panel all fogged up proved to be almost a bigger danger. When things got under control again with airspeed in limits, wiping moisture off the inside of the canopy with a gloved hand revealed clear sky. The F-5 had flown out of the tapering cloud and that funny looking airplane had followed, firing furiously. Down went the F-5 again to another cloud at 8,000 feet, staying long enough to lose the bandit.

A routine intelligence debriefing of the mission followed the landing at Mount Farm. The 14th PRS Intelligence Officer, Captain Jim Mahoney, seemed a little perplexed at the description of the Luftwaffe plane making the attack. He asked questions about oxygen supply and any lightheadedness I might have felt, but reported it all to 8th Air Force. Strange things were often seen by reccie pilots when all alone over enemy territory at high altitude. Mahoney even suggested a visit to the squadron flight surgeon, Captain Jim Savage, for a little psychiatric evaluation and possibly a trip to one of the rest homes down on the Channel. A few choice words came to mind for Captain Mahoney, but in those days Lieutenants did not talk back to Captains, or anyone else for that matter.

For the next several days the Adams name did not appear on the flying schedule, operational or test hop. Nor was the subject of the funny looking airplane raised by fellow pilots, squadron ops, or any of the group weenies. Flightline mechanics such as Sergeants Sam Quindt and Amos Ellerd were more believing, or sympathetic. First Sergeant John Mates said he might use a little help in the 14th PRS orderly room. Then 8th Air Force Intelligence put this anxious pilot right with the world again.

The 359th Fighter Group flying P-51s had reported two of these funny looking planes attacking a B-17 formation on July 28, 1944 in the Merseberg-Leuna area. They were described as fast jet/rocket powered planes with a rear exhaust emitting smoke in short bursts as though blowing smoke rings. The report had been delayed in reaching our group. Unknown to the Allies, the Luftwaffe had been testing and producing this mystery plane, the Me-163 Komet, for the past two years. The Me-163 rocket engine fighter would be seen often in the future.[13]

Notes

1. - History, 14th Photographic Reconnaissance Squadron Engineering Department, 1943, 2.

2. - Ibid.

3. - Ibid., 4-5.

4. - Roger A. Freeman, *The Mighty Eighth: Units, Men and Machines, A History of the US 8th Air Force* (London: Janes, 1986), 200.

5. - Jeffrey Ethell and Robert Sand, *Fighter Command* (Osceola, WI: Motorbooks International, 1991), 169.

6. - Yearbook, 14th Photographic Reconnaissance Squadron, 1945, 6.

7. - *Pilot Training Manual For The F-51D Mustang* (Eagan, MN: Flying Books,1989), 32.

8. - Ibid., 71.

9. - Bruce Fish to Author, letter, subject: 14th PRS History, 12 March 1995.

10. - J. G. "Jim" Fellwock, "The War Years: The Active Duty Years, 1941-1945" (unpublished memoirs, 1992), 18-26.

11. - Ethell and Sand, 165.

12. - Ibid.

13. - Col Gerald M. Adams, "Strange Encounter of a Reccie Pilot and a Komet," *Friends Journal* 16, no. 3 (Fall 1993): 29-30.

Jink, Jam, and Chaff
—The 14th Tactical Reconnaissance Squadron

14th TRS celebrates their 5000th Combat Sortie, 11 October 1968. (USAF via Parker)

After being deactivated in the 1950s, the 14th was given a new lease on life in October 1966 in response to the fighting in Vietnam. Along the way came a new name and new plane. Now designated the 14th Tactical Reconnaissance Squadron (TRS), they began flying the brand new McDonnell Douglas RF-4C Phantom II. The unit began training at Bergstrom *AFB*, Texas, and was shipped to Udorn Royal Thai Air Force

Base (RTAFB) Thailand, a year later in October of 1967. One week of Theater Indoctrination was all that was available and the squadron commenced combat flying the first week of November, 1967. The squadron was assigned to the 432nd Tactical Reconnaissance Wing along with the 11th TRS and the 13th Tactical Fighter Squadron (TFS). The 25th, 555th, 4th, and 421st TFSs were also assigned or attached to the Wing during the course of the war. The 14th jets were easy to pick out along the flightline with their "OZ" tailcode and the white "Playboy" bunny painted on the intake.

The squadron flew missions over North and South Vietnam, Laos, and Cambodia. During much of the conflict, when other units were standing down due to politically mandated bombing halts, the 14th was still flying north. By mid 1971, the 14th became the only tactical reconnaissance unit in theater. Overflights of North Vietnam ceased in January 1973, but the 14th continued operations in South East Asia until 1975, when the squadron was inactivated on the 30th of June. The 14th was considered to be the premier reconnaissance squadron in theater. As such, it received 13 campaign streamers, two Presidential Unit Citations, four Outstanding Unit Awards, and the Republic of Vietnam Gallantry Cross with Palm.

The RF-4 first flew in August 1963 and the first production version took to the air nine months later. It was developed as a natural outgrowth of the basic F-4B airframe as a replacement for the aging and slower RF-101. Although the RF-101 had a decent suite of reconnaissance equipment, most aircraft were limited to day missions when the weather was clear. The redline airspeed (maximum allowable airspeed) of the Voodoo was 600 knots indicated. In contrast, the maximum allowable airspeed of the Phantom at low level was 750 knots, although many crews saw higher airspeeds during attempts to outrun MiGs and surface-to-air missiles (SAMs)!

The RF-4 could be configured with a variety of sensors, including optical cameras, side looking radar (SLR), and infra-red (IR) cameras. There were three camera stations in the nose, each with various options of camera type and placement. The forward station could be used for day or night photography and the camera could be installed at three different angles, two looking forward and down or simply straight down. Station two, the middle station, was the most versatile. Three windows were available, two on each side of the nose and one looking directly underneath. Either the low altitude panoramic camera or up to three KS-87 still picture cameras would go in the middle station, looking left, right, and/or down. Station three, the furthest aft, carried vertical cameras only. The high altitude panoramic camera, if desired, would be carried in this aft station.

Aircraft equipped with the SLR had the antennas placed on either side of the cockpit, just forward of the engine intakes. The radar returns were recorded on film and processed after the flight. The system had an advertised resolution of 50 feet. This means that objects on the ground spaced more than 50 feet apart could be seen as two distinct targets, whereas objects closer together would appear as one. The moving target feature of the SLR was supposed to be able to detect any target moving at a speed of 5 knots or greater. The IR camera was placed underneath the Weapon System Officer's (WSO, pronounced "Whizzo") cockpit and is described as being able to produce a high resolution film map of the terrain being overflown.

At the time the 14th was flying the RF-4, they carried no weapons although before the aircraft was retired in the 1990s it was fitted with *AIM-9* air-to-air missiles. Obviously, the RF's primary defense was speed and altitude. Whether the crew flew high and fast or low and fast depended on the threat.

The AN/APQ-99 forward looking radar was relatively short ranged and was optimized for air-to-ground use, although it did have some air-to-air capability in the hands of a skilled operator. When using the radar for terrain following, the radar would alternately scan horizontally to give the WSO a ground map picture and vertically to present the pilot with a depiction of the upcoming terrain. As a concession to the jet's new role as a reconnaissance platform, the pilot's radar scope was slightly smaller than the scope in the front seat of the F-4C/D/E and moved to the left. This made way for an optical viewfinder that gave the pilot a view forward and underneath the nose of the jet.

Clark Martin

Clark Martin was one of the early members of the 14th. After his tour in Vietnam, Clark transitioned to the F-4D then got out of the Air Force in 1972. He flew several different types of aircraft in the Air Force Reserve and Air National Guard and is a Brigadier General in the New Jersey ANG as of this writing. He gives some insight into the makeup of the squadron as it was formed in the middle of the war. As with the 14th PRS of WW II fame, the 14th TRS was formed after the war started and therefore had to start from scratch in terms of aircrews. He has an interesting perspective on the squadron and its relationship with the other units at Udorn. It seems the bad feelings between the 14th and the 13th have survived the long period since WW II!

> I was in the 14th from December 1967 through August 1968, as a backseater in the RF-4C. We flew over North Vietnam, and at the time were on the 100-mission plan. Some guys who got there right before me finished their 100 in three months. After that, Pacific Air Forces (PACAF) got smart and ordered us to fly in Laos and South Vietnam as well so we wouldn't finish our commitment so quickly. In my time, one out of seven of us were shot down, mostly killed but some captured. Those who survived the shootdown spent up to five years in the Hanoi Hilton. As I recall, the 14th was formed at Bergstrom from pilots who flew the F-102 in Goose Bay and Reconnaissance System Officers (RSO) from all over the place: B-57s, RB-66s, B-47s, B-58s and a few straight out of nav school.

Backseaters weren't called Weapons Systems Officers then. But the Air Force didn't call the KC-135 and C-5 "weapons systems" then, either. We were called Reconnaissance Systems Officers, a change from the original Pilot Systems Officers where pilots were put in the back seats of the F-4. My frontseater, Paul Bertolami, started out in the back seat in Alconbury. He went through front seat upgrade while I was trained in the back seat at Shaw AFB.

Paul and I were among the first replacements to be sent to the 14th. It arrived at Udorn from Bergstrom, where it was formed, in October or November of '67. Already at Udorn were the 11th TRS, which lost four jets in one week in November '67, and the 13th TFS, flying the F-4D. For some reason, we didn't get along with the fighter guys, at least not until the 555th came over from Ubon in the summer of 1968.[1]

Amos Parker

Picking up the story of the 14th is John A. "Amos" Parker, a retired Lieutenant Colonel now living in New Mexico. He was one of the first to reply to my initial inquiries about the 14th TRS and he also provides the "meat" of the story. The first question I asked Amos, and all of the Pilots/WSOs who responded, was to tell me a little about themselves, the aircraft they flew before and after their time with the 14th, and what the general conditions were like at Udorn.

Amos Parker: Fighter Navigator. (Parker)

 I enlisted in the Air Force during the Korean War and went through basic training at Sampson AFB, New York in 1952. Because of my superior eyesight and outstanding hand-eye coordination, I went into Aviation Cadets for radar training rather than pilot training. My first assignment after cadets was as a Q-13 radar operator on KB-29 aircraft. The KB-29 was the precursor to the KC-97 and the KC-135. From the KB-29 I was sent to RB-47Es at Lockbourne (now Rickenbacker) AFB near Columbus, Ohio. After a homesteading tour at Lockbourne, I did a short tour at Plattsburgh AFB again flying B-47Es as a navigator. From Plattsburgh I was assigned to the 570th Strategic Missile Wing, Davis Monthan AFB, Tucson. Believe me, Titan II ICBM duty is everything you think it is, and worse. With great skill and cunning I managed to wiggle out of the four-year directed duty assignment in three years. Exit the world of Strategic Air Command (SAC) and enter the wonderful world of Tactical Air Command (TAC). My initial RF-4 Replacement Training Unit (RTU) was with the 7th TRS at Mountain Home AFB, Idaho. Boy, was that great! There we were crewed up, had lots of ground school and about 100 hours in the Shit Hot Phantom II, RF-4C. God, I loved that airplane. I was crewed up with Jim Pettigrew as my pilot. Jim had been a one-time co-pilot in B-47s and his last assignment was as an ROTC instructor at MIT. I've flown with lots of pilots before and since, but if ever (God forbid) I had to go to war again, I would fight to have Jim as my frontseater. Absolutely the finest!

Jim Pettigrew (left) and Amos Parker in their party suits. (Parker)

So in late June of 1968 Jim and I shipped out to Udorn RTAFB. Two crews from our class went to Tan Son Nhut Air Base outside Saigon, and the other five, Jim and I included, went to Udorn. On the way over, we stopped at Clark Air Base in the Philippines for Snake School (jungle survival training), and then on to Udorn. Jim learned at Clark, after much running around, that he had been passed over for Major.

Jim and I were put on a C-97 filled with the Air Force Band and went from Clark direct to Udorn. Because of this we missed out on the "traditional" massage in Bangkok. The entire 14th met us on our arrival at Udorn and we were promptly told no one in the squadron was patronizing the Officer's Club. Seems the Squadron Commander had been thrown out for burning a paper Christmas tree in the Club! The big rush from Clark to Udorn, and the reason for us missing our massage, was to relieve a crew that had finished their hundred over the North but could not leave until their replacements arrived (us).

The squadron had a very diverse background. The crewmembers were former altitude chamber instructors, B-57 drivers, ex-supply types, many ex-missile types. Very few folks had reconnaissance or fighter backgrounds. Fran Houlk, who was later killed by a commie terrorist on his way into town, and Fletcher Cook, were exceptions and had flown RF-101s out of Don Muong Air Base, near Bangkok.

The crew hootches generally had two people to each room who were almost always members of the same crew. Most room doors were painted appropriately. The field grade crewmembers (majors and above) generally lived in trailers with two bedrooms in each trailer and a connecting latrine. The crew hootch was built of teak, had a common latrine, and a common room where we used to gather, drink, and tell fighter pilot lies. During the day our maids would use the common room for shining boots and shoes and washing our clothes. Late at night a gecko lizard occupied the common room. If the gecko made its usual noise, someone was "down." Someone down, as explained to me early on, did not mean they had landed. It meant they had either crashed or been shot down.

Example of a hootch door at Udorn RTAFB. (Parker)

The crew chiefs were a great bunch of guys and were they ever dedicated. They were always waiting for you in the parking area on your return from a mission. If you could give them a "thumbs up" as you taxied in, their smiles were a mile wide. Aircrews and ground crews were very close, and it was not uncommon for aircrews to take an hour or so off from a party and deliver several cases of beer to the flight line.

Amos Parker and his crew chief. (Parker)

Our attire was typical of the period. G-suit of course and the 500-pound survival vest. The vest contained two radios, extra batteries, extra ammunition, first aid kit, blood chit, and tree lowering device (in English, 150 feet of rope). Most of us carried extra water in our G-suit pockets. The extra bottles were tough to come by and several of us wrote home for plastic baby bottles. I carried a white handkerchief wrapped around the front buckle of my harness to clean my glasses of sweat. Most of our work was at altitudes below 500 feet for a time in Laos. The RF-4 air conditioner was not worth a damn at low-level and high humidity. It would fog the canopy and cause predictably disastrous results. We kept it off during low-level. On my left hip was a standard issue Air Force survival knife. On my right hip was a non-issue Smith and Wesson Model 28 .357 Magnum. Carrying my own personal sidearm was very illegal. About once a month I received a very nasty letter telling me I was violating the Geneva Convention by carrying the .357. Into file 13 it went. The only violation was the hollow points I carried. I had smuggled the gun over to Udorn and managed to smuggle it back to "the land of the Big BX" (the U.S.) in my baggage.[2]

Jim Pettigrew in his flight gear. (Parker)

Since Amos had started his flying career in KB-29s and eventually transitioned to RB-47s, I was curious to hear about his impressions of his first fighter.

What did I love about the RF-4? First, I could see outside! In almost all other aircraft I've flown it was like being locked in a closet. Second, I had a stick and throttles. I got pretty good at making Ground Controlled Approaches (*GCAs*) but Jim would not let me make a landing or do any refueling. Lots of Guys in Back (GIBs) did these exotic things, but again, my superior hand-eye coordination won out. Later on, in the F-4D, I got pretty good at close formation. Third, it was fast. Every once in a while, in the RF, we would get frustrated with just taking the gomer's pictures and would sonic boom them. Fourth, the Inertial Navigation System (*INS*) was a navigator's dream. Who would believe you could read ground speed or track from a dial? Lastly, the radar was outstanding once you got used to a *forward sector scan*. It was powerful and could be a great mapping radar, in the right hands.[3]

Rear cockpit of the McDonnel Douglas RF-4C. (Parker)

One of the fighter pilot traditions that still survives today is the party suit. It is a lightweight one piece jump suit, usually cotton or polyester, that is similar in appearance to the Nomex flame retardant flight suit the crews normally wear. The party suit is worn to squadron functions such as going away parties, or anytime a celebration is in order. I asked Amos about the 14th TRS version.

> Our party suits were maroon and we had a white Playboy bunny with a red "14" over it engraved on the right breast. It also had a 12-inch black Phantom patch on the back. Many different patches were earned for different missions. For instance, you couldn't wear the Night Owl patch until you had flown nights (very unnatural and very scary). Of course other criteria applied for the River Rat, Brown's Lake Official Guide, Phase Tester, Yankee Air Pirate, or Atlanta Falcon patches. Every squadron also had a "party girl" who wore the squadron party suit, a replica of the suit we wore except with a skirt instead of our "flying bags," and took care of her squadron when any member was in the bar. Our pooying (girl) was named Nan and had "Shit Hot RF-4C" engraved on the back of her panties. It took very little coaxing to get Nan to show her shorts!

Ron McQueen, Tom Foster, Jack Hazlet and Amos. (Parker)

The party suits would accumulate a lot of patches over the course of a combat tour and each had a story. I got the Atlanta Falcon patch during the last three months of our tour at Udorn when Jim and I participated in a test program. The original concept was to marry a single fighter (F-4D) to a single reccie bird. The fighter was to be a fast Forward Air Controller (*FAC*) and find targets to strike. The fighter would direct the reccie bird to take pre-strike photos, then put in an air strike and finally have the reccie bird take post-strike Bomb Damage Assessment (BDA) photos. Occasionally, if the fighter had more strike aircraft than it could handle, the reccie bird would act as a fast FAC and put in the strikes. The fighter's callsign was to be "Falcon" and the reccie bird's callsign was "Atlanta." Of course the original concept went down the tubes in a big hurry and what finally occurred was much more productive.

The system evolved into each aircraft going its separate way immediately after takeoff, the fighter finding targets to put strikes in on immediately and worrying about the BDA later. The recon guys would roam anywhere around Steel Tiger (northern part of the Laotian panhandle) and sometimes into North Vietnam (Route Pack 1) taking pictures of whatever struck their fancy. Jim and I called it "free lance photography!" Occasionally we would put in a strike if the Falcon had too many strike aircraft to handle. Of course this presented a problem for awhile as 7th AF, the guys in Saigon who were directing and "winning" the war, would not authorize a reccie to carry white phosphorous (WP or "Willie Pete") rockets to mark the targets. Of course we cheated and loaded night photo flash cartridges (carts) on Atlanta aircraft. I don't remember the specific details and specs for the carts, but the big ones went off with about 10 million candlepower and closely resembled an 85mm explosion. The cart left a sizable cloud of smoke after it exploded. As a result our directions to the strike aircraft went something like this: "See our smoke? O.K., hit directly under it." Really unorthodox!

The results were spectacular for both Falcon and Atlanta crews. Most targets developed by both reccie squadrons, the 14th and 11th, were developed by Atlanta crews. Most of the successes were due to the lack of involvement from 7th AF and the crews ever-increasing familiarity with the area. The crews got lots of time, usually two and a half hours of flying with two tanks of gas, with two days of flying and one day spent helping the photo interpreters to figure out what we had taken pictures of. We carried 1,000 feet of film and most of the time Jim and I returned to base (RTB) with *bingo* film (empty). Naturally, only those flying as Atlanta or Falcon were entitled to the Atlanta Falcon patch.

Brown's Lake was an area and small lake perhaps 30 miles southwest of Dong Hoi, as I remember, and named after either a "Full Bull" colonel or lieutenant colonel intelligence officer named Brown who developed the target. It was a hot area and we lost several fighters in the immediate vicinity. Anyone working the area, either reccie or fighter, was entitled to a Brown's Lake Official Guide patch.

Immediately after the bombing pause in November 1968 a program was initiated to test the gomers in this phase of the war, hence "Phase Tester". Initially only the recon birds flew these missions. They were primarily designed to gather intel, but also to see if the gomers would shoot at us. Of course the little brown bastards did shoot, and their aim was just fine! Our reaction was to then escort the recon flights with fighters. If the guns came up the fighters would roll in and take out the guns. That was great if you had a point target, but if it was a line of communication (***LOC***) like Highway One from Dong Hoi to the De-militarized Zone (DMZ), the guns at the start of the run would shoot at you and the fighters would take out the first guns. But the gunners for the remainder of the strip, sometimes 90 miles long, had a field day with no threat from the fighters who had expended all of their ordnance on the first gun.[4]

My next set of questions to Amos dealt mainly with training and tactics. I am very familiar with the day-to-day operations of a fighter like the F-16 and I have seen a 180-degree shift in training and tactics just since the Cold War ended in the early 1990's. So, knowing that tactics change, and because there aren't any tactical reconnaissance platforms in the USAF anymore, I wanted to know how Amos went about getting the pictures without getting shot.

As far as tactics go, first let me tell you a little about recon. One out of every two RF-4s built had Side Looking Radar. It was very high resolution and you could fly to the left or right of your target and still obtain the intel. It was a very large scale image, meaning it covered a very large area. We didn't use it very often. We also had a so-so IR sensor that transferred the images to film. Again, you could stand off from the target, but we seldom used it to take a target. We used it instead, mostly at night, to keep track of the aircraft position and make it easier for the interpreters to interpret the night photos. I'm a bit hazy (Alzheimer's attack!) about specifications and names for most of the cameras but will give you my best "guesstimate."

We had a low pan (panoramic) camera with a triangular, rotating lens that took a photo from the nine *o'clock* horizon to the three o'clock horizon. The high pan camera was essentially the same idea. Its coverage was only 45 degrees either side of the center line instead of the low pan's 90 degrees. It had a large format and focal length and we sometimes mounted it in the forward oblique position. We used two different vertical cameras, one with an 18-inch focal length and the other with a 36-inch focal length. Sometimes we mounted the 18-inch vertical camera in the left or right oblique position. This gave you a stand off capability that was seldom used, i.e., the ability to look under jungle canopies and camouflage (if you were low enough) and into caves.

By far the most common method of taking a target was to directly overfly it and use the vertical camera. During daylight missions most photos were taken visually with a radar backup, meaning the target was identified using our optical sights and eyeballs as opposed to the radar.

At night it was almost always a radar show. Occasionally on a night with a full moon and a target in a relatively flat area you could take the target visually. On a point target you would drop a photo flash cart directly over the target and the flash of light from the cart would trigger the camera. Guys with little teeny weenie gonads would drop only one cart and hope it was dropped directly over the target. Guys like Jim and I, with average-size family jewels, would drop three carts attempting to bracket the target. The big kids with solid brass equipment dropped five carts. The night targets were assigned by 7th AF and most often had the same time on target (TOT) every night. The ferries, fjords, and assorted interdiction points in southern North Vietnam and Laos were usually run from the same direction and the same altitude because of camera limitations and 7th AF restrictions. As soon as the first cart went off, the gomers had a damn good idea of where the aircraft was and where it would be. After the second, there was no doubt of where the bird was. It was an awful lot like shooting a sitting duck. At the very least, after the first cart went off things got rather spectacular.

In RTU we practiced pop-ups. They were a lot of fun and you came screaming across the deck at maybe a hundred feet to a point adjacent to your target, then popped up to 16,000 or 17,000 feet, took your photos, and dropped back to the deck. We never used the pop-up in Southeast Asia (SEA). It was developed as a tactic against SAMs and had ceased to be used up North by the time Jim and I arrived at Udorn.

There were quite a few similarities between planning a photo run and planning a bombing run in bombers. Both required a straight in approach to the target, an Initial Point (*IP*), and a prediction of what you would see on the scope. On a point target you could *jink* vertically but had to remain on the planned track. One guy in the Triple Nickel (555th TFS), after observing a reccie run near Vinh, said he guessed everyone had their moment of truth. He was referring to the fighter's inability to jink once he had his pipper on the target versus the reccie bird's inability to jink left and right during a photo run.

Normally in Laos we were restricted to flying above most small arms, 3,500 feet. Altitude restrictions were waived for Atlanta Falcon flights and we could go in at any altitude we damned well pleased. Let me tell you it was like giving a couple of kids a license to steal! I've never had so much fun flying. I've found flak traps while flying at 600 knots and 50 feet. The gomers would take 55 gallon fuel drums that had been shot up and put them in a big stack, surround it with camouflaged small arms and AAA in an attempt to sucker in some strike aircraft. If the drums had bullet holes, and were in a neat stack, it was an obvious flak trap.

There were some disadvantages to low-level, high-speed work. One was the problem with the air conditioner I described earlier. Another was learning how to observe different features. Obviously if you only observed items at the three or nine o'clock positions they would be nothing but a blur at very low level and very high speed. If, however, you started to observe the same object at the 11:30 or 12:30 positions, and followed it through to the three or nine, it was amazing what you could observe. For instance, the bullet and cannon holes in those fuel barrels.

Another disadvantage was the increased vulnerability to small arms. If at low level you followed an LOC for any length of time, you would be in deep kimchee as the gomers would call ahead and tell their friends to start shooting straight up and we would fly into the ground fire. Best to keep jinking and cross the LOC at close to a 90-degree angle, or follow it only for a very short distance. If you went fast enough and low enough and didn't follow an LOC or a predictable pattern the gomers did not have the field of vision or reaction time to shoot at you, let alone hit you. If you got too low and too fast you would "run away" from the cameras though, leaving gaps between the individual picture frames. If you had gaps, then no 3-D photos and probably lost intel. The advantages of low-level, high-speed work in Laos sure outweighed the disadvantages, besides it was lots of fun. With the side oblique camera you could fly to the right or left of a target and get photos without flying directly over the target. This was sometimes better than a vertical photo because if you were low enough the photo would show what was under the jungle canopy.

Almost all of our missions were flown single ship, hence the motto "Alone, Unarmed, and Scared Shitless." The exception was well after the bombing pause, when we were escorted by fighters on day missions over the North. The fighters had a tough time keeping up with us. We had much better performance and were not hampered by lots of garbage (bombs, that is) hanging on the wings. The fighters had to go AB to keep up with us when we were in Mil.[5]

Flying fighters is obviously a high-risk proposition. Training Rules (TRs) have been established and numerous regulations are in place to help mitigate this risk while at the same time allowing the pilots to train realistically. Many of the TRs are written in blood. In other words, somebody died either because the rule didn't exist or was broken. Amos was one of a couple of pilots who mentioned that losses occurred which really can't be called "combat" losses.

Bob Smith and Ray Boucher had to shut down one engine shortly after take off from Udorn. Unfortunately, the other engine was locked in AB and they could not get it out. We listened to the whole show over the squadron radio and marveled at Bob's control of the situation even with the extraneous advice and B.S. offered by the command post. Bob and Ray punched out over the controlled bail-out area. Pedro, the rescue chopper, picked up Bob from a rice paddy in a few minutes. Ray spent most of the night in a tree arguing with Pedro about how to get out of the tree! Pedro wanted Ray to use his tree-lowering device, and Ray wanted Pedro to get him out with their jungle penetrator. The entire discussion was over *Guard* so we heard the whole thing. Ray finally won, and a good thing too. The rope on his tree-lowering device was too short and Ray already had a hairline fracture of his neck from the ejection. In those days, we used a 40mm cannon shell to punch the seat out. The rocket was not yet installed. If Pedro had not pulled him out, he would have completely broken his neck and been killed.

One guy used the 5-6 lockout switch which locked out fuel cells 5 and 6 for a better center of gravity (CG), thus giving him better maneuverability. You had to be careful when doing this as you could trap 2,000 pounds of fuel in the wings if you didn't keep an eye on things. He and his GIB discovered their error when they flamed out on GCA final and had to eject!

The 14th Ops building was about 1,000 feet off the runway and you could look out a large front window and observe all the activity on the runway. About September of 1968 (I had been there less than a month) a huge rainstorm hit and as it passed through, the tower switched active runways. Both an RF-4C from the 11th and an F-102 were airborne at the time and I was staring out the front window looking at the rain. The RF-4C made its approach and was landing on the current active while the Deuce, which had lost its radios, made its approach and was landing on the old active. The two met about the middle of the runway and the RF swerved to his right while the Deuce swerved to his right. A slight dent in the RF's left wing was all that happened to him and he managed to stay on the runway. The F-102 was not so lucky and he went off the side of the runway at about 130 knots. A large road grader was parked along the side of the runway and, you guessed it, the Deuce rammed it. I saw the resultant explosion and ball of flame from the squadron window. The Deuce was of course totaled and the force of the impact ripped the ejection seat and pilot from the airframe and threw it 100 feet down and onto the runway. When the meat wagon showed up the medics were afraid to unstrap the jock and loaded the seat, pilot and all, into the ambulance. Believe it or not, the Deuce pilot did not so much as scratch his nose and was back flying within a week. All I could think of was that I had somehow been transformed into a comic strip. I was there, I saw it, but I still don't believe it.[6]

Since I have never dropped bombs in anger and have never been shot at while flying, I was really interested to hear about how Amos handled it and what it was like. This is the type of information you just can't get in training.

In early October 1968 Jim and I had been flying combat for about 60 days. Most of the missions were in Steel Tiger and Route Pack One and we weren't sure if we were being shot at. There were no SAMs this far south of Hanoi or in Laos at this time and small arms fire is not particularly easy to see on a clear day, particularly if there are no tracers. A couple of times we thought the gomers were using 37mm on us but the white puffs looked a lot like small white clouds and they were at least a thousand feet below us. We felt like we were being shot at but couldn't see it.

Then we started flying nights. I'm here to tell you that flying combat at night, whether or not you're being shot at, is not only scary as hell but is down right unnatural. As a result, the old timers treated the nighttime new guys (FNGs) to lots of suggestions and help. In fact, the old guys took on the appearance of mother hens, with the FNGs as the chicks. Our first night target was a strip about three miles long and about 20 miles west-northwest of Dong Hoi. It was a ferry route and would require at least five photo flash carts to get the strip. It was an easy target to find because of the land-water contrast that would show on the radar but would present lots of opposition because of its length and the AAA in the area. The mother hens gathered around and the general opinion was, "Everyone takes this target going east to west, from feet wet towards Laos." Being the rebel I was, and because repetition could get you killed, I said, "Jim, lets take it from west to east, headed from Laos towards feet wet. If we get it, I'd rather go into the gulf than the mountains." Jim agreed and that's the way we did it. I think we used seven carts, we got the target, and did not have a single round fired at us, that we could see.

To say the least, we were both feeling a bit cocky, and the second night our target was a point target, a ferry crossing about 30 miles west-southwest of Dong Hoi. Again the mother hens gathered and the advice was, "Everyone takes this target using the Co Ta Roun as an IP going south to north." Unfortunately, there was no other good way to take the target because there seemed to be no other adequate radar returns to use as an IP. Well, at least we would only have to use three photo flash carts. That night was a real revelation.

When the first cart went off the whole world lit up with *ZPU*, 37mm, 57mm, and at least a dozen BB guns shooting tracers. It was if the whole world had exploded. Jim immediately said, "They're shooting at us!" I was so damned scared that all I could do was answer him, "Press on" and stick my head back in the radar scope under the theory that what you can't see, can't hurt you. As soon as the third cart went off, which seemed like three hours later, Jim went full AB and started a climbing turn towards home. About five minutes later we were level at 25,000 feet and headed home. Neither Jim or I had said anything since the target run and I finally got my breath back and said, "Jim, those S.O.B.s were really shooting at us!" Jim said, "SHOOTING AT US!" and threw the aircraft into a right slice! As soon as I caught my breath I told him I meant back at the target! We leveled off and headed home. On every single mission after that we saw ground fire, even during clear days over Laos, and never again doubted that we were being shot at.[7]

Anyone who is familiar with the war in Vietnam knows that Hanoi was not a good place to fly over. Every conflict seems to have one or two targets that are notorious for their defenses. I asked Amos about some of the other trouble spots when he was with the 14th.

> One place you did not want to visit was Tchepone. It was a major transshipment point in the central part of the Laotian panhandle. Jim and I had heard about it within two weeks of arriving at Udorn. A Triple Nickel bird was shot down there and a huge search and rescue (SAR) effort was underway. I don't recall if they got the guys out or not but it definitely indicated that Tchepone was not a milk run.
> Several months later Jim and I drew Tchepone as a target. We flew the point target from north to south and took quite a bit of AAA. When directly over the target the aircraft shuddered and we felt a thump on the underside of the fuselage. Jim and I just knew we had taken a hit, but all instruments read O.K. About halfway to the second target our fuel consumption grew alarmingly so we aborted and returned to base. On our way home we requested a chase plane and he informed us our engine bay doors were open. The doors had not been properly fastened when we departed Udorn and that was the jolt we experienced. Of course, the additional drag caused our fuel consumption to go to hell.
> On a lighter note was a reccie run over Tchepone with Al Chase. Al was a "ring knocker" from West Point and although a bit straight laced, he was a nice guy and a good jock. It was sometimes frustrating not to be able to strike

back at the gomers. As a result we sometimes did dumb things and were always plotting some sort of revenge. Sonic booming the bad guys was one result.

For a while we had talked about dropping toilet paper on the gomers, and Al Chase and I decided that today was the day and Tchepone was the place. Right after the Intel briefing we laid out four rolls of toilet paper on the flight-planning table and invited everyone to write a message. Some of the messages that I remember were, "You'll wonder where the Yellow went, when we thermo-nuke the Orient," "Ho Chi Minh likes little boys," "F—North Vietnam," and at least another dozen equally astute comments. The main idea was that the gomers would not know what it was and their intel people would spend large amounts of time trying to figure out what the toilet paper was and what the writing said. Maybe the intel report would make it all the way to Ho Chi Minh or General Giap and the messenger would be executed. In any event, Al and I loaded the four rolls into the speed brakes and in due course dropped them over Tchepone. Never did hear anything about the drop.

Sam Nuea was another place that was not very popular with Jim, myself, and most of the other reccie troops. Sam Nuea was a provincial capital in northeast Laos, about three miles west of the North Vietnam Border. For a while Jim and I held the record on the "Nit Noy" record board for the most AAA fire in one picture frame. Thirty-seven rounds of 37mm and 57mm over Sam Nuea.[8]

Lastly, I asked Amos to recall some of the memorable missions he flew with the 14th. Like any good fighter pilot, not all of Amos' stories involve flying!

Around March of 1969 I was flying a daylight mission with Art Krenzel, another *Zoomie U.* graduate. He was a young Captain and a helluva nice guy. Art had been doing some test work with an F-4 unit out of Ubon that was trying out the new smart bombs called *Paveway*. Art had a high pan camera mounted in the forward oblique position. The idea was to get pre- and post-strike photos of the Paveway target. If we photographed the target in a 45-degree dive the high pan camera would give a good imitation of the strike pilot's pass. Unfortunately this would require the pre- and post-strike photos be taken from the same dive angle and heading as the strikers. This was a great way to help the strike pilots, but a dumb way to ensure survival. The target was a small wooden bridge about 30 miles southwest of Sam Nuea and was really quite a difficult target to hit with a bomb. Art and I rolled in on the first pass and got our pre-strike photos. Halfway down the chute I spotted and commented on a 37mm going off at our six o'clock. A couple minutes later the two F-4s from Ubon showed up. We briefed them on the ground fire and they rolled in, one aircraft lasing the target and one making the drop. I don't remember why, but it took them four tries before they were able to release. But what a drop it was. It was a shack and totally wiped out the bridge. It was our turn to roll in, the sixth pass with the same dive angle and heading. DUMB! Two thirds of the way down the chute we took a hit with a 37mm and ZPU. Believe me there was no doubt that we had been hit. The 37mm blew off our centerline tank and the ZPU put shrapnel in our engines. I put our INS on *homeplate*, told Art the INS was on Udorn, and said to take up a heading of 200 degrees. I then came up on Guard and started calling a Mayday. No one answered and by that time Art came up and started calling. I went over to *HF* and contacted the command post at Udorn and gave them our position and status. After a couple of minutes I looked up at a compass that was reading 065! When I stopped rattling around in the rear cockpit and got Art turned back to 200 he told me he had gotten hold of an Air America chopper that gave him a heading to channel 85, Lima site. The only problem was the Lima site had been overrun by the gomers six months previously! We landed back at Udorn 40 minutes later, sans Utility and Primary hydraulics and the HF radio. We took the barrier and later drank a lot of beer. Art told me he was damn glad I had that big .357 with me, as he felt we were going to have to walk out of Laos. The maintenance folks told us we had about five minutes left on the engines. The Paveway troops at Ubon seemed very pleased with the photos and Art and I had a few more gray hairs.

About May of 1969 Jerry West and I were flying an Atlanta mission. We had an 18-inch side oblique camera mounted and were looking for something interesting near Sam Nuea. For some long-forgotten reason we ran down the ridge line there on a south-southeast heading with the side oblique mounted on the right side. We had no idea of what we had until the photo interpreters showed us the photos we had taken. There was a series of caves halfway down the ridgeline. Standing in the mouth of one of the caves were three people. All appeared to be Caucasian and two were dressed in one-piece suits (flying bags?) and one had on dark slacks and a white shirt. There was all sorts of unusual activity around the caves and at the foot of the ridge line. The photos engendered a lot of high level interest and a blow up of that photo with the folks in the cave was fully two feet high. I'll never know for sure but I suspect, and intel suspected, a POW site. I do know that a "no-bomb" zone was placed around the area shortly thereafter and it was still there when I returned in 1972.

Ike Derrick was a Captain frontseater, passed over for major, who was approaching a hundred missions over North Vietnam and a ticket home in May of 1969. Ike was arguably the nicest, most popular guy in the 14th. His high spirits, ready smile, and good cheer accounted in great part for the high morale of the 14th. When the Majors' list came out in 1969, Ike was on it. The night before the major's promotion party, Ike, in true aviator fashion, was celebrating his promotion at the bar. He was standing at the bar with his foot on the bar rail when a squadron member, who shall forever remain nameless, grabbed him, lifted him up, and turned him around. It was an expression of pure joy at Ike having made major. Unfortunately, when Ike was turned, his foot slipped between the rail and the bar and the turn broke Ike's ankle. It was a compound fracture and Ike was scheduled to be *air evac'd* to Clark early in the morning after the party.

The next evening, the night of the promotion party, the entire 14th assembled in the front hall of the Udorn hospital while Ike was wheeled out in his bed to say "***Sawadee***" to the guys. Numerous bottles of champagne were consumed and before the squadron was thrown out of the hospital, the squadron Commanding Officer (CO) asked if there was anything Ike wanted. Ike responded by saying that when Ralph Findly, the 432nd ***DCO***, was shot down over Dong Hoi and recovered, he was presented with a 37mm shell casing. Well, Ike said he would sure like to have a piece of that damned bar rail. The squadron was then asked to leave the hospital so we adjourned to the club and the party.

Entertainment was furnished at the club in a large area adjoining the bar. At 2100 hours, in the middle of the show, the entire 14th left their seats and went to the bar. The bar, of course, was deserted as everyone else was watching the entertainment. There was only one bartender, who we proceeded to drive crazy. The bar was "L" shaped and most of the squadron members assembled at the corner of the bar. If you listened real close, you could hear a hacksaw at work. When the two-foot section of the bar and two uprights were removed, the squadron promptly returned to the promotion party. No one caught on to what had just taken place. The bar rail and two uprights were sent to town the next day, mounted on red velvet and framed. The brass plaque mounted underneath said, "Presented to Ike Derrick, shot down by this 37mm bar rail at Udorn RTAFB, 16 May 1969."

The whole enchilada was sent to Ike at Clark Air Base and I heard it now hangs over his fireplace. The entire operation went so smoothly that two weeks later one of our guys was telling a 555th jock about it. He didn't believe it until he walked over to the short end of the bar and discovered the missing section of rail. He thought it was so Sierra Hotel that he proceeded to rip up the remainder of the rail!

One last war story. On the road into Ban Kari Pass from North Vietnam there was an interdiction point we commonly called the Dog's Head, named that because the road wound around a small hill that resembled a dog's head. When we were flying as Atlanta Jim and I usually took this target by running south-southeast down a valley between the Dog Pecker and the steep karst that defined the Animite Mountains. We would go down this valley at about 540 knots and 300 feet. When we were abeam the target we would do a climbing roll to the north-northeast. The target was probably a thousand feet above the valley floor and we would level about 500 feet above the target and get our pictures. We never saw any ground fire when we did this, but for some long forgotten reason we decided one day to roll in from 4,000 feet, level at 1,000, get our pictures, and leave. When we leveled at 1,000 a ZPU opened up on us. We finished our run, did some more free-lance photo work, and hit our tanker twice. Finally we rolled in on an interesting bit of karst about 20 miles southeast of Mugia Pass. A 37mm opened up on us and Jim started a sharp pull up from the gun. Now Jim is a big man and when we pulled up from the gun we pulled about three or four Gs. When Jim's G-suit inflated it shoved against the speedbrake button on the throttles. When that happened we dumped hydraulic fluid overboard and lost the primary system. Seems that we had taken a hit two hours earlier from that ZPU at the Dog's Head and the round had severed the hydraulic line coming from the speed brakes. If we hadn't actuated the brakes we would never have known we were hit. Of course we called a Mayday and headed towards home. An hour after delivering the film to the photo interpreters, the 555th launched a flight for Mugia Mountain and when they left the target they had counted over 70 secondary explosions. Made it all worthwhile.

Jim Pettigrew on the flightline at Udorn. (Parker)

Your last combat mission was, of course, a big deal. You were greeted at your aircraft, given a bottle of champagne, dunked in a pool, hosed down by a fire truck, then convoyed to the squadron for a party. That night the dinner was usually a side of beef paid for by the guys flying their last mission. The standard comment was, "Well the war is over, the railroad built, and all the Thais laid."

Sawadee celebration for Tom Foster, Bob Hust, Big Jim Pettigrew, and Amos Parker. (Parker)

In August of 1969 I shipped out of Udorn with 175 combat missions, eighty over the North. I was assigned to my second love, F-4Ds of the 9th TFS, 49th TFW, Holloman AFB, NM. In 1972 the whole wing, four squadrons worth, deployed to and re-opened Tahkli RTAFB. This time I got to kill some of the little brown bastards, instead of just taking their picture. Another 125 missions.[9]

Howell Jones

A fighter squadron is made up of anywhere from 25 to 35 pilots, or in the case of the RF-4, crews. Not all of these actually work in the squadron. Roughly 25% are "attached" to the squadron. That is, they do their deskwork in another unit on the base and fly with the squadron as their schedule allows. These can be evaluators, pilots who work at one of the headquarters organizations, or most often members of the wing leadership structure. The pilots in wing leadership positions, usually lieutenant colonels or colonels, rotate their flying among the squadrons assigned to the wing to keep a perspective on how things are going "in the trenches." Howell E. "Hal" Jones flew with the 14th from June 1971 to August 1972. He initially worked as part of the wing leadership staff and later went on to command the 14th. His experiences are valuable in that he has a perspective on operations in the entire wing and he got to see a bit of the "big picture" surrounding the day-to-day operations at Udorn.

> When I arrived, Lt. Col. Reeves was the squadron commander and Maj. Ken Fields was the ops officer. Upon my arrival at Udorn, Ken, two squadron pilots and a friend from my B-58 days met me. I was given first-class treatment, which was a 14th standard welcoming. My friend informed me that I was getting the best job in the wing, Wing Chief of Operations and Tactics. He had just been promoted to colonel and was transferring to Da Nang. The operations and tactics shop was made up of three reccie crews, three fighter crews, and a wing weapons officer by the name of Bob Lodge. Bob was a 28 year old major and a graduate of the Air Weapons School located at Nellis. I soon learned that Bob planned all of our strikes into North Vietnam. The weapons and tactics shop was responsible for planning the missions and training the crews in the wing. We also ran the fighter alert operations.
>
> Around the first of July, 1971, the wing assistant director of operations (*ADO*) was transferred and I was assigned that job awaiting the new guy to show up, which took about two months. At this time we were flying a lot of

heavy sorties into the North. Our reccie jocks increased the airspeed to 540 knots as there was lots of AAA and SAM sites. Unfortunately, at 540 knots the film was blurred. We learned that the nose vibrated at that speed but was O.K. at 600, which became more or less a standard speed for targets in high threat areas.

Around the first of August we had, I believe, four fighter squadrons plus the 14th at Udorn, for a total of over 170 F-4s on base. The wing director of operations (*DO*), Col. Epperson, was called back to the States for about five weeks and as there was still no assistant to take his place I was given the job of DO until his return. During this time we flew one of the Bob Lodge strikes to Hanoi. We had all 170 birds with engines running and taking off. Soon Tom Gorman, the new ADO, showed up and we became fast friends. He shared his large two-bedroom trailer and we remained roommates for the rest of my tour.

While I was playing DO, two State Department guys showed up wearing dark suits and ties, but carrying their jackets, a good move. They rolled out a large map of northwest Laos and told me they would like us to take photos of this large area. I told them we didn't have the resources but if they could send me another reccie squadron we would give it a whack. They were not happy so I sent them to the planning shop, the photo lab, and the squadron commander and told them if they found out anything different than what I told them I would be glad to talk to them again. I never saw those two guys again!

Around September the fighter guys were losing a bunch of people dropping sensors. During this time, the wing *executive officer* came into the office and told me that the Boss wanted to see me and Bob Lodge, right now. We went to the commander's office and he was stuttering badly and just pointed to Charlie Gabriel's office (the vice-wing commander) and said, "Fix it!" When we went into Charlie's office, Bob talked, the vice-commander nodded, and I took enough notes to fill half of a legal pad! Bob fixed the problem and we lost no more planes dropping sensors.

About this same time Charlie moved up to wing commander and Jerry O'Malley became the Vice-Commander. Charlie and Jerry made an outstanding team. Bob Lodge checked Jerry out in the F-4D. Both were well liked and respected. Jerry Grimes became squadron *operations officer* and Ken Fields moved to maintenance liaison officer. Later I learned that the senior and experienced majors essentially decided who would move to squadron operations and the outgoing guy would run maintenance. This system worked exceptionally well.

I believe it was early Fall when we started the daily morning *weather ship* runs to Hanoi, before sun up. All went well for awhile. But the fighter jocks decided that it was not a great deal to be flying formation in the dark, in weather, down among the trees with a reccie jock flying the terrain following radar (TFR) and heading to Hanoi! The reccie jocks were on time and on the money with no problems, which was standard reccie ops, but it became difficult to get the fighter guys airborne. Early one morning, the wing commander walked up to me, put a finger in my chest and told me that he was damned tired of getting his ass chewed every morning for the weather ship flight taking off late. One did not have to be a rocket scientist to understand that the commander was highly pissed. Back to see Bob Lodge. We decided to put six birds on alert and start all six, taxi four and hold two at the alert facility. Manning and starting six jets in order to launch two was a lot of work, but we had no more late weather sorties. The fighter guys were not pleased!

I should note here that around September 1971 Harry Brown became commander of the 14th. Harry came from 7th AF and had been commander of a B-58 squadron while I had been ops officer of a sister B-58 squadron. Harry and I had a "royal battle" over who would become the Commander of the 14th. Charlie Gabriel made a great decision that Harry and I would get a four-month tour each as commander. I should also note that Harry was my mentor, stiff competitor, and life-long friend. Harry passed away somewhere around 1979. I miss my good friend Harry Brown and think of him often.

Around the first of the year, 1972, the 14th started picking up two to three missions each day that were directed by the President. Running the railroads from the Chinese border on each side became regular missions and going downtown became more than a daily mission. It seemed that most of the missions could be described as "heavy" and things became more difficult as time passed.

I became commander of the 14th around March 1972. I had noticed that a few of the senior pilots seemed to be flying all of the "heavies." Late on my first day, I was briefed on the next day's sorties. The same guys were flying the heavies again. I directed the ops officer to divide the squadron into two groups, those who were qualified as flight leads and those cleared to fly as wingmen. I told him this applied to "heavy" missions too and to put my name at the top of the following day's missions. I felt that every qualified crew should fly their share of the tough missions and that I was not about to play God.

One of the missions directed by the President was to run strips over Hanoi at 420 knots and 4,500 feet using two reccie birds and four fighter escorts. Jack Rollins, the 13th TFS Commander, was the flight lead for his squadron. After the briefing, Jack came up to me and said his guys were not going as it was a suicide mission, an obvious observation as Charlie had been on the phone for about an hour trying to get the mission canceled. I called my good friend Wayne Fry, the 555th "Triple Nickel" Commander, and told him the 13th had walked out on us and I needed a flight of four. He asked how soon and I said, "About 30 minutes ago." It seemed that as soon as I hung up the phone in walks Wayne, suited up and with his flight of four! He merely asked where we were going. I had the intel guy brief him and the six crews left to start engines. As we were taxiing out we got word that Charlie had the mission canceled. The "Nickel" would go anywhere with us. They and the 14th were tight.

Somewhere about this time we lost a crew over the North. We flew the area several times each day searching for the guys. After about three days Charlie told me that 7th AF had directed that we cease all search for the downed guys. After 25 years I guess it's O.K. to confess that I "forgot" to pass that directive on! On the eighth day one of our senior captains organized a full rescue and they were brought out by the Jolly Greens. What outstanding warriors these people were. I hope we gave the Silver Star to that outstanding captain.

No story of my time would be complete without a few more words about Bob Lodge who flew with the "Nickel."

Charlie Gabriel had asked Bob to extend for his third tour. Bob was an outstanding officer, pilot, and warrior. He was our chief MiG killer with four to his credit when a MiG-17 and MiG-21 teamed up on him north of Hanoi and shot him down. The backseater (Roger Locher) bailed out but not Bob. He had told me months earlier that if they ever got him he would ride it in. Bob had planned and directed too many large-scale missions over the north. He had also dueled with "Col. Tomb" many times. Bob was our top guy. He taught me the fighter business and taught many other crews for that matter. Steve Ritchie was a young captain and flew many missions as Bob's wingman. Bob was like a brother and also a good friend. I miss him.

At Udorn, I learned quickly that while SAC wrote everything down and led from the top, TAC guys wrote nothing down and led from the bottom up. Bob Lodge and I started writing down the important things. Bottom up leadership is far superior when you have people who are the best in the world at what they do.

Even though I cherish my days in the B-58, it is clear that my years flying with the 14th were the best years of my life. I became a better pilot, a better officer, a better Commander, and a much better man. I value the 555th plaque that hangs on a wall in my office, but when I look at the 14th plaque that hangs on the same wall I am reminded that the 14th was clearly the top squadron at Udorn. The "Nickel" was second, and the other three squadrons a very distant third through fifth. Charlie Gabriel once asked me, "How is it that we have four fighter outfits and one reccie squadron on the base, and you reccie jocks run this wing?" I answered, "A reccie jock is just a real smart fighter pilot!"[10]

Chuck Munroe

Although technically outnumbered and outgunned, the North Vietnamese Air Force (NVAF) had quite a few advantages of its own. Any student of airpower history knows that for many reasons, the USAF and USN had their hands full for a time with the slippery MiGs. One of the biggest advantages the MiGs had was the ability to fight over their home turf. Many times, even if the USAF F-4s had the positional advantage, they just couldn't afford to stay around and fight. Given the high cost of the F-4 when compared to the MiG, and the fact that the F-4 had a two-man crew, it would be a shallow victory at best to shoot down a MiG and then run out of fuel! This left many fighter and reccie crews with little choice when faced with a MiG other than to turn and run for home. Not glamorous, but as they say in the corny flying movies, "It is better to retire and to fight another day than to push a bad situation." Chuck Munroe flew with the 14th around the time that Hal Jones was the squadron commander and he relayed to me interesting encounter he had with the NVAF.

> I'm sure that most of my 14th TRS squadron mates who, like me, were frequently shot at in SEA attribute making it through that war in part due to the fine plane we flew: the RF-4C. It was a wonderful piece of war-fighting equipment that had speed, agility, and the strength to withstand abuse.
>
> One day I won't soon forget was one morning in early 1972. I was flying a weather reconnaissance mission in preparation for a coordinated Linebacker strike into the Hanoi area. I was the flight lead and had two fighters on my wing for protection. We went into the North across the Black River several times, looking for acceptable weather conditions. Finally, after two air-to-air refuelings, I was able to report that the weather had broken. We were egressing into Laos when ***Red Crown*** came up, saying that

we were being intercepted by two MiG-21s! First the MiGs were at 21 nautical miles (NM). They had a 30-40 degree angle-off intercept. In no time they closed to 12 NM. We jettisoned centerline tanks and accelerated from 480 to 540 knots. But, very quickly, the MiGs closed the gap to six NM. We got rid of the remaining wing tanks and accelerated to 600! They kept closing. That goes to show you what good angle-off will do for you!

Next, Red Crown said, "They're arming their missiles." Earlier, we'd been told when the MiGs dropped their tanks. By now our situation was becoming more tense than fun! When the MiGs closed to inside three, I informed my "escort" that I was heading for the weeds and the fight was theirs!

In the weeds is where the RF-4C really showed its strength. I nosed the beast over and headed for the hills, selecting full AB. We had been flying just high enough to keep in contact with Red Crown, about 4,000 to 5,000 feet above ground level (*AGL*). Soon, I was amongst the trees and the low clouds. Between concentrating on the TFR and the radio, I neglected the airspeed indicator, which hadn't seemed very important because I knew I wanted a lot of "smash!" I knew that in a tail-chase I would win. When next I spied the airspeed indicator I was amazed. We were going 940 knots and still accelerating! The redline was 740 knots! Soon, I got the beast harnessed.

Well, we suffered no damage from the MiGs or from the airspeed. In the past I'd often heard that you could accelerate the RF-4 until the engines ripped out. Now, I knew it to be fact. What a machine!

An irony on that mission is that after seven to eight minutes of going like hell for home I finally decided that it was safe to climb and slow down. I pulled up above the low clouds and, to my amazement, my fighter "escort" was three miles in front of me! From that time on I was sure that reccie pilots must have their own guns and missiles![11]

Brian DeLuca

In April of 1972 an amazing rescue effort was underway in North Vietnam. A high-ranking officer by the name of Hambleton had been shot down and it was imperative that he not fall into enemy hands. This saga is well told in the book *Bat 21* and the movie by the same name. Brian DeLuca was a pilot with the 14th at the time and he remembers the time well. Brian retired as a lieutenant colonel and is working on Boeing's part of the F-22 as this is written. He was with the 14th from July 1971 to July 1972.

On 4 April 1972, I was airborne on a reconnaissance mission as aircraft commander of an RF-4C Phantom out of the 14th TRS from Udorn. Coming off a tanker, I was summoned to cancel my planned mission and proceed to the DMZ area and await instructions in the air. I was advised that since I was the best immediately available long range navigation (***LORAN***) equipped fighter qualified to "Pathfind" (lead instrument bombing), I was being diverted to support a search and rescue. My task was to lead waves of assorted fighter-bombers to bomb release points that would be sent to me by radio. When connected, these points formed a ring around Bat 21. We dropped through total overcast, using LORAN coordinates developed from photos taken by my unit during clear weather for other purposes, but now very useful for this rescue effort. I was "on station" for about two and three-quarters hours with my own dedicated tanker. I flew about a

30-mile long racetrack pattern and picked up a fresh wave of bomb-laden USAF and USN fighters on the downwind leg. I briefed them in the air and gave them a "get ready" and then a, "5, 4, 3, 2, 1, pickle," call at the release point. They peeled off and left and I turned downwind to get the next group. These groups comprised mixes of F-4s, F-105s, and A-7s, whatever could get up there and stay in formation with bombs on board. On the final run-in, with about 30 seconds to go until release, they really pulled in tight and then went up and away when the bombs came off. It was quite dramatic! Sometimes we had to adjust our speed to reach a best compromise for the different types in the formation, plus figure and put in real-time corrections for the wind. But otherwise, that is what we were supposed to be able to do. If you do the math, 2.75 hours of 30 NM legs plus four to seven wingmen per drop, that is a lot of bombs! I hope we did some good. At the time, I didn't know the significance of who we were covering, nor the full scenario of what was going on down on the ground. We were just told to, "Pathfind better than you ever did before. There's a friendly down there!"

Several days later, with the weather still bad with low ceilings and rain, I was selected to be the deputy lead of a formation of six. We had two reccie leads (Dan Kelly and me) plus four attack Phantoms, to drop suppressant *on Hambleton and his area* to quiet it so a chopper could safely get in. A previous attempt on another day resulted in the loss of the chopper and crew. We reccies would lead because we were better trained and qualified to do the low-level visual navigation at tactical speed. If Dan's plane aborted, we'd still go with the four and me. The mission was cancelled when the ceiling went below 100 feet, as reported by Bat 21. Otherwise, we were set to go.[12]

Brad Johnson

Brad Johnson, a WSO with the 14th from October 1972 until October 1973, got his commission from ROTC at Washington State University. Charles Debellvue, who finished the war with six kills and was later the base commander at Misawa in the early 1990s, was in his ROTC class. Brad served one tour in Vietnam and then went on to fly RF-4s in England before going on to navigator Test Pilot School. He eventually wound up at Eglin AFB, Florida, testing new systems. My first question to him was about his background, training, and what he thought about the RF-4.

> I was born and raised near Seattle, WA near the SEA-TAC airport. I went to Washington State University and got my commission through the ROTC program. Since I was in Electrical Engineering and had good grades I got a regular commission. After graduation I delayed going on active duty to complete a Master's Degree. In my ROTC class was Buck Adams, who set a speed record flying an SR-71 from London to New York in 1975, and Jim Fleming, winner of the Congressional Medal of Honor. One of my roommates in Nav School was Charlie DeBellvue and my RTU pilot retired as a one star.
>
> Before going to Udorn, I had gone through RTU at Bergstrom AFB, TX and then stayed there for about three years as part of the 4th TRS and the 45th TRS until October 1972. At Bergstrom, I became proficient at low-level day and night navigation. Most of our flying in RTU and in the squadron was single ship. We flew formation only when going to the tanker and when having

standardization-evaluation (Stan Eval) checks. The only air-to-air training we received was two or three rides in the RTU to have high and low speed yo-yos demonstrated.

The thing I liked best about the RF-4C was that as a backseater I actually had a mission, at least at night. For a night mission, radar was the prime method of navigation. We had a terrain following radar that gave the pilot an *E-squared* presentation and the backseater a ground map picture plus or minus 15 degrees either side of true ground track. We used a more normal plus or minus 45 degrees presentation when we were above 2,000 feet AGL. In SEA when I was there we had to stay above 4,500 feet but the trouble was that some of the hills really went above that fast. The RF-4 also had an INS that had about a four NM per hour Circular Error Probable (CEP). This meant that if you told the system where it was in terms of latitude and longitude, within an hour there was a 90% chance that it still would be accurate to within four NM. It did have a nice feature of telling you your true ground track. This really cut down on flight planning time since we didn't have to convert anything to magnetic headings.

Our training in the States consisted of flying low-level routes, doing pinpoint targets, area covers, and LOC reccie. We had low, medium, and high altitude target requirements. Daytime navigation was primarily visual with radar as backup. At night it was all radar. Daytime sensors included low, medium, and high altitude cameras. For nighttime we also had an IR system that covered 3,000 feet either side of the flight line when you were flying at 2,000 feet AGL. We also had a side looking radar that I found was useful for showing geologic formations and not much else. We also were equipped with photo flash cartridges that could illuminate the ground well enough to take pictures from 5,000 feet at night. We did not use them very often in SEA because they tended to say, "Here I am, here I am." to anyone interested in tracking an easy target at night.

The thing I noticed when flying the F-4 at Eglin after the war was that all the low-levels ended up at a bombing range, and there was a strong tendency to use preplanned low-level missions. When I flew at Bergstrom and then at Alconbury immediately after my tour we always had new targets to photograph along the low-level route.[13]

Some of the other pilots/WSOs had commented on the diverse makeup of the squadron. I was curious if the varied backgrounds of the crewmembers continued as the war progressed.

By 1973, the war had been going on for a long time and there was a general realization that it was not going to continue forever. To encourage voluntary participation, a lot of career opportunities revolved around a SEA tour. It was the only way to change aircraft. My RTU pilot was originally a KC-135 copilot. He did not graduate that high in his pilot training class and got a KC-135 instead of a fighter. By volunteering for a SEA tour in the RF-4 he automatically became an aircraft commander. The bad thing was that his classmates, who graduated pilot training higher and chose F-4s out of UPT, were put in the pit as copilots and were still there when he was an RF-4 aircraft commander. In my case, I wanted to go to school at the Air Force Institute of Technology (AFIT). However, a SEA tour was required before an AFIT tour would be considered.

> Any type of command assignment needed a previous SEA tour.
>
> For the younger guys, none of it really mattered. It was really an adventure for them. Where else could you be in the thick of combat one minute and a few hours later be relaxing at the club, having a good meal with your buddies? So, for whatever reason, we were all there. There just should have been a filter to catch the ones who really had no business being anywhere near combat. The only restriction I remember was that you needed to have 25 combat missions in Laos or South Vietnam before being sent North. On my 26th mission, I was headed for downtown Hanoi.[14]

In a conflict that lasts for a long time the tactics are bound to change. The enemy learns from his mistakes and our victories just as we learn from his. Brad saw a war six years removed from the one that Amos Parker saw. Had the procedures and tactics changed much?

> At the time I was with the 14th, we were known as the "Bunnies" and lived by sayings such as "One pass and haul ass," "Unload and go," "Jink, jam, and chaff," and "There's only two kinds of people, ones who have been lost and ones who will get lost." Back then a recon formation was two RF-4s working in the same general area! There was even a song that mentioned us. It started with, "Throw a nickel in the grass and save a reccie pilot's ass, and you'll be saved." Never did learn the rest of the words to the song. When we really did have to fly as two-ships, the meat of the briefing was, "I'm lead, you're two. If you fall behind me you're going to get your ass shot off." The major threat to us was small arms which was why we needed to stay above 4,500 feet AGL. "Unload and go,"

was so important because of the limited air-to-air training we received. Since our only armament was two six-shot .38s our best defense was to run like a scared rabbit. Rumor had it, however, that some of the guys did get rather good with the centerline tank. They were able to consistently hit one of the islands in the Mekong when it came time to get rid of it before going up North. We did not lose any crew from my class. However, the class that graduated before ours lost a nav, Don Shay, and the class after ours lost a pilot and nav. Don had been one of the groomsmen when my wife and I were married. They never found Don's crash site. The other crew ran into one of the isolated hills in the Mekong Delta.

When I got to Udorn, I had to learn how to operate the LORAN. I knew the theory and had used some really old LORAN sets in nav school. The only instruction on using it was the Aircrew Aid and advice from other navs and pilots in the squadron. I was at Udorn when one of our squadrons bombed the Da Nang *TACAN* off the air. The lead pilot thought the nav had the bombing point in the LORAN. Instead, the nav had the TACAN coordinates set in. Needless to say, the next version of the LORAN in the F-4 (ARN-101) would not let you bomb navigation points!

In August of 1973 a new IR system was being tested out in the RF-4C. I was selected as one of the WSOs to fly with the new system. These missions were typically flown at night, which is why I was selected. The war was a 90% daytime operation at the time and since a few of the WSOs and I had previous night experience past the RTU level we got the job. These missions were difficult to plan since they could last up to five hours. Each waypoint had to be determined and then plugged into the LORAN during flight. I think only about 10 to 15 points could be plugged in at a time and we usually had 50 or more points for a mission. Since these were the days before data transfer modules it made for a busy flight. One night we were flying in Laos along the Ho Chi Minh trail, which was by then a highway. I did not have time during the first half of the mission to put in the points for the second half. The weather was bad, so I spent my time watching the radar to make sure we didn't make a turn into something that was not fluffy white. Anyway, we orbited at altitude while I put the rest of the points in the LORAN. We started our descent to 4,000 feet MSL toward our start point along the Mekong River. I was watching the radar so I could pick out the river. I remember telling my pilot that the return did not look quite right. It finally dawned on me that I was looking at the north side of the Bolivians plateau, which went up to 5,500 feet! I told Mac to pull up and climb. At that point we were less than one minute from impact. I misread the coordinates on the map by 15 minutes and had not had time to double-check my work. I was so shaken I asked Mac if we could call it a night and head home. He agreed. That was the last time the IR system was flown on a night mission in Laos. The results were not very impressive.

At 4,000 feet AGL, the system only had about 1,000 feet of coverage. Since the trail did not go where the map showed it, it was rather hard to get coverage when you were just going from point to point using coordinates picked from a 1:250,000 map.[15]

One of my objectives when I started this history was to give the guys in the current squadron a feel for what combat was like. So far, we've heard some pretty impressive stories of AAA and SAMs and a few encounters with MiGs. Again, since the war was so long and the threat constantly evolving I asked Brad to describe his experiences with the North Vietnamese defenses and if he noticed any trends or lessons to be passed on to the current generation.

I only remember getting shot at once, at least where it could hurt us. This time we were flying a mission to the east of the Bolivians along the Mekong River. Our mission was to take pictures of a "suspected" road. As we were descending toward the start point, I noticed dust to the east of our position. I pointed out the dust to my pilot, Maj. Ray Ford. We decided to take a little detour and take a look. As we were turning, I saw stars to the starboard of the aircraft and thought I should take it easy on how much I was drinking at night. The dust was being stirred up by 15 trucks going down the Ho Chi Minh trail. We took pictures of the find and called in the location to the C-130 Airborne Command and Control Center. As we started to line up with our IP I looked down and saw a rather large sunflower winking on and off down below. I then realized the earlier "stars" were actually tracers and what I was then looking at was the business end of a 23mm AAA piece. We did some jinking and were quickly out of range. After we were done taking pictures of the "suspected" road, Ray wanted to see if we could give the gunner a scare by flying over the site at 600 knots. I told him we had already broken the "one pass and haul ass" rule that day and maybe we should leave well enough alone. It later turned out the North Vietnamese were putting supplies onto barges and moving the cargo along the Mekong and then into Cambodia.

My roommate at Udorn told me that on his first flight over Laos he had seen a flock of white birds when they were flying over a place called the Catcher's Mitt. He mentioned it to the pilot, but the pilot did not seem too concerned. When Bob was at the bar that night he was telling the story to some other guys who were rather amazed that he did not realize the white birds were 57mm tracers. I guess the gunner was also getting his *dollar ride* that day. Another new WSO arrival had a similar experience. The pilot heard him muttering something about what he was seeing. When asked what he was talking about, the WSO pointed out a spiraling vapor trail that was coming toward them. It was a shoulder fired IR missile! It ran out of energy before it was a threat to them. I guess the point is that none of the new people really had any idea what AAA or missiles would look like.[16]

A second objective of this history is to pass on some advice to the "young bucks" flying today. I asked Brad about the things he saw in Vietnam that he thought were mistakes and could have been done better. It is interesting to note that he echoes the earlier sentiments about people doing stupid things because "this is combat" and he elaborates on his point that there should have been a better process in place to keep out the pilots who were there just for their career.

MiG kills seemed to be a hot poker in everybody's pants at Udorn. During the year I was there the wing lost 32 F-4s and was credited with shooting down 31 MiGs. Not bad until you considered that an F-4 costs four times the amount of a MiG. All of the wing losses were listed as "combat losses." One of these "combat losses" was a guy wanting to get home fast so he was in full blower (afterburner) below 10,000 feet and decided to pop the speed brakes so he would not go supersonic in Thailand. He got into a PIO (Pilot Induced Oscillation) and he and the WSO had to step over the side.

Another was a single ship sent to Da Nang with fresh flight suits for the troops sitting alert. A first lieutenant with four hours sleep in the last 24 hours was the pilot and a flight surgeon was in the pit. Everything went O.K. until they were given a letdown into Da Nang. It seems the level off altitude got left off the letdown instructions. Two weeks later a scar was found on a mountain side north of Da Nang. Another problem was running out of JP-4 after getting a MiG but before getting home.

I'm sure the wing had some real combat losses, but there seemed to be many losses that didn't really have much to do with what the other side did. A big part of the problem was the attitude of our wing commander. He called himself "Press On" Smith. He managed to run into his flight lead before taking the runway once and also managed to launch a *Sparrow* when he was supposed to be clearing his 20mm. His comment to lead when the Sparrow took off was something like, "Don't worry, it's mine," as the Sparrow became the new formation leader. Needless to say, with such flying performance and frequent requests for new F-4s, good old "Press On" was the first out of ten wing commanders *not* to make general.

The 14th lost one aircraft during that time. It was hit by a SAM. That loss probably could have been avoided, given 20/20 foresight. This mission required the RF-4 to fly a straight and level course at 10,000 feet while taking photos of the terrain. LORAN data was collected and recorded on the film. The photos were processed and

LORAN data generated for selected points on the pictures. The RF had two F-4 escorts. Anyway, the mission that day went through a SAM ring with the RF being in the lead. What went on in the RF is not clear. The crews of the F-4s saw SAM activity on their radar homing and warning (*RHAW*) scopes but didn't say anything to lead. At some point the RF started a gentle descent. I believe two SAMs were fired. When the first SAM went through the formation the F-4s decided it was time to take some positive action. I think the second SAM got the RF. The pilot was killed and the backseater punched them both out. His name was Hector Acosta. He managed to evade capture for about two days before being picked up by the North Vietnamese. At least two rescue attempts were made to get him out. On the second attempt, the Jolly Green was shot up, one engine was knocked out, the pilot incapacitated, and the rest of the crew wounded.

The investigation of the loss found that the F-4s RHAW systems were programmed differently than the RF's. I believe it was concluded that the RF system would not have responded to the signals that were being displayed on the F-4 scopes.

I had flown with Hector's pilot the day before. Our mission was near the DMZ and as we were going feet wet to hit a tanker our RHAW scope lit up with SAM launch indications. I told the pilot we needed to start moving around until we could figure out what was going on. His comment was that we shouldn't worry because we were more than 20 NM from the coast and were outbound. I kept checking six real hard anyway.

Even earlier, I had been talking to Hector's pilot in the bar. He was a senior major and was more than eligible for retirement. Since I was a bit older than my squadron mates (I was 29 at the time), he thought I would be sympathetic to his ideas. One of the problems with doing recon of a road is what to do when the road makes a 90-degree turn. When you're doing 540 knots ground speed you lose a lot of coverage with a 45-degree banked turn, since the cameras take pictures of what is under the belly of the aircraft. One solution was to slap 60 degrees or more of bank in and pull hard on the pole, then get straight and level as fast as possible. This resulted in some loss of coverage but not as bad. Another technique was to pull the aileron-rudder interconnect circuit breaker. This took out a rudder movement restriction and enabled full rudder deflection at any speed, allowing you to put the aircraft into a hefty skid while turning the aircraft to the new heading. As a result the road would be completely covered. The skid was also rather uncomfortable, but it got the job done. Doing a 270-degree turn was dumber than dirt since it took you over the same bit of real estate twice and also wasted gas. Hector's pilot though it would be much better if you pulled the aircraft up, let the speed bleed off, make the turn, and then descend while picking up airspeed along the new heading. This maneuver had airspeed, altitude, and heading all changing at the same time. He thought this would make a gunner's problem very difficult. I just let his idea pass, thinking he was not really serious.

The RF crews were not immune to screwing up. Since we had such good cameras we were always proud to take "happy snaps" of anything special. Just before I arrived at Udorn a reccie crew was working with an OV-10 FAC. The reccie crew tried to take a picture of the OV-10 with the vertical camera. In the last shot the OV-10 upper fuselage covered the whole frame. After the impact the RF was able to land. The OV-10 crashed and the pilot ejected. After that it was a BE-NO (as in "There will *be no* more…") to take an air-to-air photo with aircraft cameras.

F-105 Wild Weasels photographed from a 14th RF-4, well before this was a Be-no. (Parker)

After leaving the 14th TRS, I went to the 1st TRS at Alconbury, England. I was told that I was not combat ready and would have to go through an exhaustive upgrade to meet USAFE combat standards! I amazed everyone by upgrading in about two months. Some younger guys had been there nearly six months and still were not upgraded. I think they were confusing being combat ready with being able to fly in Europe and being able to pass an Operational Readiness Inspection (ORI). At Udorn we had one week of ground school and then got a "dollar" ride. After that it was a check ride every day. It was called combat. If you could order a drink at the bar at night you passed! One of the fellows who had done two SEA tours went to Bergstrom AFB after his second tour. He also had trouble becoming "combat ready". Seems he had an attitude problem with trying to maintain plus or minus five knots on an instrument approach. For the last two years all his training was to keep the smash up and not worry about speed, then get on the ground as expeditiously as possible. With training, he eventually became "combat ready."

Before I graduated from RTU my instructor, Gordy Edwards, told me to always keep an eye on that cockpit instrument that did not need electricity or any other outside help to operate, the not-very-accurate "whiskey" compass. He told me to always make sure that where I thought we were heading and where it said we were heading were about the same. When he was at Udorn, one of the reccie crews came off their target in the North and put homeplate in the INS on the nose. Remember, the INS had a drift rate of about four NM per hour. Well, in this case they realized the INS was about 40 degrees off. They were headed for China. I think they realized their mistake and turned toward the south. They ejected over Northern Laos but were never found.

I was Gordy Edwards' last student. After our class graduated he retired. That was in 1969. I can still see him limping across the flight line at Bergstrom to fly a Functional Check Flight (FCF). I asked him one time why he kept flying and he just smiled.

Even though a lot of aircraft were lost during the SEA conflict there was a statistic that I thought was really interesting. In combat **no one** ever went in with a sick bird. Maybe they stayed with a dying bird so they could be someplace else when they ejected. In the peacetime Air Force then it was a common occurrence that the crew would try to save a situation that could not be saved and would end up getting killed. If there were ever a lesson to be passed on it would be to not wait too long to use the nylon letdown device. Any landing you can walk away from is a good one.[17]

John Heide

Closing out the saga of the 14th in Vietnam is John W. Heide. He served at the very end of the conflict and has a unique perspective on the last days of the 14th TRS.

Since my tour was during the latter stages of the USAF's presence at Udorn, November 1974 to July 1975, I had a unique, though not too harrowing, tour. I was a brand new major in the summer of 1974 when I got my orders at Bergstrom to replace the current ops officer of the 14th. Delays placed me on station in late November long after my predecessor had left. The interim ops officer's first name was Darryl, but that's all I remember.

Combat support missions were still being flown over Cambodia and South Vietnam with the altitudes varying from a minimum of 4,500 feet up to 25,000 feet, depending on what the intel troops were pumping out as to what the threat was. Because of the shaky nature of the remaining US presence, the edict had gone out that no reccie would fly at a threatened altitude. Our missions included surveillance of the convoys bringing relief to Phnom Penh, Cambodia, reccie of all major roads and pig-trails in Cambodia, real time reconnaissance of the Phnom Penh pull-out, and surveillance of the fall of the South Vietnamese Army and the VNAF. Additionally, the unit was involved in the Kho Tang Island flareup over the Mayaguez incident.

In mid-April, 1975, I led the last USAF tactical reconnaissance mission over South Vietnam. The objective was to photograph the land and water escape routes from Saigon to the coast. I remember the mission for two reasons. The first was that it was long and cold, about four and a half hours. It was flown at about 25,000 feet and included two aerial refuelings at Hickory Track over Ubon. My air conditioner froze full cold, which at first seemed to be a good deal. However, when I went numb from my butt down, it started bugging me! As a side note, my ice-water bottles were still frozen solid upon RTB.

The second reason I remember the mission was that I had a front row seat for the VNAF battle for Bien Hoa. The west perimeter had been overrun and the A-37s were taking off to the east, climbing out and bombing the bad guys on the west end of the field, and landing back to the west. After that mission, reccie was grounded for out-of-country missions and the fighters got a chance to screw up the actual pullout. And they really did! I was the night supervisor of flying (*SOF*) on the day they did their thing. They scattered more rockets and bombs on paddies in Thailand than anything else.

My final business with the squadron was the re-deployment of the birds to the States on July 7 through 13, 1975. The prep and departure to Guam as an interim stop went well with 15 of our RF-4Cs and three to five E-models tacked on. Mike C. Sheen was my GIB and it felt rather good with all of us with the Playboy bunnies on the splitter vanes and a lieutenant colonel fighter puke taking a back seat to this young major reccie pilot! He had an F-15 assignment waiting for him.

Guam was nice and uneventful for us except they didn't have enough support equipment to get us all to our next stop, Hickam AFB Hawaii, at once. I led the first contingent to Hawaii and "suffered" through four days on the beach prior to departing for Bergstrom. The bunnies came off at Hickam due to their unofficial nature. The final leg on July 12th was uneventful except that Mike and I had to divert into George AFB, California because some SAC puke ratted on the fact that our refueling door was frozen open. We got into Bergstrom on the morning of the 13th to be met at the plane by Brig. Gen. George Edwards, TAC Inspector General. Usually only bad things happen when a high-ranking officer meets you at your airplane after you've landed. We breathed a sigh of relief when we found out that they had arrived the night before and his car was the only one available!

One other item of note was that the only squadron casualty during my tour, other than hepatitis, was a lieutenant who came out of his hootch across from the Club with his T-shirt still up over his head and went spread eagle into newly strung razor-wire. It seems that the engineers and police had reduced the cantonment perimeter overnight and not notified anyone![18]

Notes

1. - Clark Martin to Author, letter, subject: 14th TRS history, 10 June 1994.

2. - Amos Parker to Author, letters, subject: 14th TRS history, 8 April 1994 through 5 April 1995.

3. - Ibid.

4. - Ibid.

5. - Ibid.

6. - Ibid.

7. - Ibid.

8. - Ibid.

9. - Ibid.

10. - Howell Jones to George Engel, letter, subject: 14th TRS history, date unknown.

11. - Chuck Munroe to George Engel, letter, subject: 14th TRS history, 22 September 1997.

12. - Brian Deluca to Gerald Turley, letter, subject: Bat 21, 27 May 1997.

13. - Brad Johnson to Author, letter, subject: 14th TRS history, date unknown.

14. - Ibid.

15. - Ibid.

16. - Ibid.

17. - Ibid.

18. - John Heide to George Engel, letter, subject: 14th TRS history, 18 August 1997.

Vipers in Japan—The 14th Fighter Squadron

14th TFS at Misawa Air Base Japan in the Spring of 1993. (USAF)

As the F-16 was starting to come into the Air Force in significant numbers in the early 1980s, the 432nd Tactical Fighter Wing (TFW) was re-activated and the 14th once again became a force to be reckoned with. The squadron was re-designated the 14th Tactical Fighter Squadron "Fightin' Samurai" on the 5th of June 1984. Activated on the 1st of January, 1987, the squadron started flying the General Dynamics (now Lockheed) F-16C out of Misawa Air Base, Japan. The squadron was originally placed on the northern tip of Honshu for two reasons. The first seems obvious and that was to help Japan defend herself in the event of any hostilities. Second, since the Japanese constitution forbids any sort of offensive capability, the Samurai were placed there as a means of counter-attacking any strikes by the Soviet Union. The location in the northern part of Japan was very well chosen, with Misawa Air Base being as close to three major Soviet airbases as it is to Tokyo. For these reasons, and the requirement to keep North Korea in check, the 14th did not get to participate in Operations Desert Shield and Desert Storm.

The Samurai were one of the first operational squadrons to fire the AGM-88 *HARM* missile from a Viper. They were also the key factor enabling the 432nd TFW to be one of the first units declared operational with the *AMRAAM* missile.

Sadly, in a misguided attempt to preserve the heritage of what was mistakenly believed to be a more historically significant unit, the 432nd Tactical Fighter Wing was inactivated in the winter of 1994 and the wing re-designated the 35th Fighter Wing. The "Tactical" had been dropped from the squadron and wing titles a year previous in another misguided attempt at re-organization and political correctness. This politically correct atmosphere also saw the change of tail codes from "MJ" to "WW," to reflect the Samurai's new mission as the successor to the F-4G in the Wild Weasel role.

Insignia of the 14th TFS. To reflect its new role, a Samurai warrior on a lightning bolt replaces Bugs Bunny on a P-38. Note that the Samurai is using a side stick, just like in the F-16! (USAF)

When the 14th TFS was re-formed, it was paired yet again with the 13th TFS at Misawa flying the General Dynamics F-16C. Initially equipped with the Block 25 version, the squadron quickly upgraded to the Block 30 "Big Mouth." General Dynamics, and then Lockheed, used Block numbers to distinguish between various versions of the F-16 when the changes did not warrant a new letter designator. For example, the Block 25 was the initial version of the F-16C and had a Pratt and Whitney engine. The Block 30 saw the introduction of the General Electric F-110 engine into the fleet. The early Pratt and Whitney engines, while they were a revolution in jet engine design, were always considered inadequate for the F-16. They remained so until the Pratt and Whitney -229 engine was put into the Block 52 in the 1990s. After the initial production batch of Block 30s, Lockheed found that by widening the engine inlet they could get an extra 3,000 pounds of thrust out of the motor, thus the "Big Mouth" moniker. Whether by coincidence or design, the 14th was given the big mouth jets just as the 14th PRS was given special treatment in WW II by being assigned Spitfires and Mustangs.

The squadron's mission was mainly long-range interdiction with an additional tasking for air defense. When the squadron transitioned to Block 50s in the spring of 1995, the primary mission changed to Suppression of Enemy Air Defenses (SEAD or Wild Weasel), while the requirements for interdiction and air defense remained.

In the early days of the squadron, the threat was the Soviet Union and the squadron had planned to fight in place in the event of a major conflict with the Soviets. Since the fall of the Soviet Union, the squadron has had to adapt to the USAF's new vision as an Expeditionary Air Force, meaning they could be deployed at short notice to fight anywhere on the globe. Numerous three and four-month deployments to Saudi Arabia and Turkey since the end of Desert Storm have borne this out. Like the rest of Pacific Air Forces (PACAF), the Samurai also stand ready to pound North Korea in the event the uneasy truce on the Korean Peninsula breaks down.

Misawa Air Base looking east. The coastline is about 2 NM from the end of Runway 10. (Author)

The Samurai are the only credible SEAD assets in the Pacific Theater and as such have to be ready to counter a wide range of threats. This includes not only the very same SA-2s that the 14th saw in Vietnam but also the sophisticated SAMs that the Soviet Union developed during the 1970s, 80s and 90s. These can be found in places such as China and the Former Soviet Union.

The first pilot I spoke with joined the 14th immediately after they were re-formed at Misawa. I have deleted the pilots' real names and replaced them with their respective call signs to protect those who are still actively flying. The Khobar Towers incident of 1996 and the recent bombing of the U.S.S. Cole proves that American servicemen still are not immune to terrorism.

Sluggo

I became a member of the 14th Tactical Fighter Squadron in July, 1988. I was one of a group of first time "Samurai" lieutenants (Spanky, Frosty, Squirt, Sledge) who were solely trained by the initial cadre of the 14th. It was a great time to be at Misawa Air Base, Japan. The squadron was about a year old, since re-commissioning that is, and we had great leadership. We were flying the small mouth Block 30 F-16 at the time but soon transitioned to the big mouth jets.

My first real memories of the 14th are of endless exercises. The wing had failed the *Phase I* Operational Readiness Inspection (ORI) and we were doing a Phase I or *Phase II* Local Operational Readiness Exercise (LORE, pronounced "Lorry") about every other week to prepare for the Phase II ORI coming up in November, 1988. It was during my first Phase II LORE that I got a wake-up call on how dangerous the fighter business really is. I was flying on the assistant operations officer's wing, on the third day of the exercise, when he had an engine failure and subsequently ejected in the mountains over central Japan. There were two of us trying to run a Search and Rescue Combat Air Patrol (*SARCAP*) in a small valley below a 500 foot overcast. The flight lead, Mumbles, had turned his Guard receiver off when Vido jumped out and I found myself talking to Vido on the ground, relaying to Mumbles that he was okay and wondering what this hideously loud sound was that I couldn't seem to get to go away. That sound happened to be the low speed warning horn! I was in full afterburner, about 400 feet above the ground, in as tight a circle as I could fly so I could keep Vido in sight and doing about 150 knots. It was pretty exciting for a non-mission qualified wingman on his tenth sortie in his first real fighter squadron. This mishap didn't even slow down our exercise schedule. We continued this hectic pace through the ORI, which, thank God, we passed.

After that endless period of exercises, we got into a pretty routine schedule in the 14th. Home for two months and then *TDY* for one month. We continued this pace until I left the Samurai in July of 1991. During that period we spent about eight months in the Philippines (*Cope Thunder* and *Combat SAGE*), two months in Alaska, one month in Australia, one month in Okinawa and one month at Nyutabaru Air Base. I can say with conviction that during the period of 1989-1991 there was NO better fighter squadron in the world than the Samurai. We went everywhere and kicked everybody's ass and still hit the target.

While many fighter pilots say their first tour was their best assignment and that squadron was the best, I was truly blessed by being in the 14th Tactical Fighter Squadron for my first tour. I made friends for life, especially my usher partner Sledge. I got to fly and lead sorties that guys usually don't get to see until Fighter Weapons School. I truly believe the reason Sledge and I did so well at Fighter Weapons School was that nothing at that school could intimidate us. We had already seen it and done it in the 14th.

My second tour in the Samurai was an emotional roller coaster. Most of the time I wanted to kill somebody, occasionally it was myself but most of the time it was the squadron or wing leadership. I returned to a squadron in March of 1995 that was a mere shadow of the squadron I had left only four years earlier. Most of that was due to incredibly poor leadership at the squadron (though the current squadron leadership was good with GAK and

P.K.) but especially at the wing level. The wing commander had completely destroyed the wing's tactical capability and a good deal of the morale. There were good things at the wing, like Nordo, the operations group commander, who knew where he wanted to take the wing tactically but the ominous "wing commander cloud" overshadowed everything. It was sickening to walk into my old squadron on a Friday afternoon and be offered an O'Doules (non-alcoholic beer) because the wing commander would not allow alcohol in the fighter squadrons.

I began my second tour at Misawa Air Base assigned to the operations support squadron and attached to the Samurai for flying. During that period I was in charge of converting the squadron from the Block 30 F-16 to the Block 50 F-16 and the SEAD mission. Six months into my tour and three months into the Block 50 conversion I was made the chief of weapons and tactics at the 14th. I was the squadron weapons officer for about a year and a half. It was very rewarding to see the light come back on and the new Samurai become the terror of the skies again. Only six months after I began upgrading the first Samurai to the SEAD mission we went to Green Flag for the first time in Samurai history. Green Flag is similar to the *Red Flag* exercises held at Nellis AFB, but with special emphasis placed on electronic combat. I was very proud to be a part of the unit that broke every Green Flag record for SEAD effectiveness after only a couple of months of training. We followed that up with a *Combat Hammer* exercise where again the Samurai set the new standard of excellence.

I gave up the weapons shop to become a flight commander in the Samurai and the project officer for the 14th's first combat tour since South East Asia. We deployed to

Operation Northern Watch (*ONW*) from March to July 1997. While at ONW the Samurai set the standard in everything they did. We took over the SEAD mission from the 52nd Wing at Spangdahlem and went about updating everything done tactically at Incirlik Air Base, Turkey. During our time at ONW the Samurai set in place the tactical operating procedures that were used in the December 1998 bombing campaign in Iraq and subsequently Operation Allied Force. It was very rewarding to receive letters from the commanding general of ONW thanking the Samurai for changing the face of ONW.

I left Misawa Air Base in April of 1998, knowing that the "Terror of the Pacific and Protector of the 13th" was back.[1]

Dano

Dano arrived in the 14th about the same time as Sluggo's first tour and left Misawa in 1994. He typifies the warrior spirit that has always set the 14th apart from its peers. The stories he remembers are a good example of that attitude.

> Misawa's close proximity to the Russian mainland added an extra measure of realism to our home station training and at times afforded the unique opportunity to meet our enemy in person. On practice missions to Wakkanai, Hokkaido's northwestern corner, we could look north across the La Perouse Strait and see individual buildings and warehouses along the Sakhalin Island coastline. Occasionally, Soviet EW radar from the Kurils would spike our radar warning receivers as we worked targets on Eastern Hokkaido. At times, we would stumble across Soviet naval vessels that routinely patrolled in close

proximity to the Japanese shoreline. Russian fishing vessels were often encountered as they made port in Hachinohe harbor to trade at the massive fish market in nearby Hachinohe City. Often times we would hear a Japanese *GCI* controller over Guard issuing warnings (in his best Russian language) to Soviet aircraft flying in close proximity to Japanese airspace. Three Japanese Air Self-Defense Force (JASDF) Mitsubishi F-1s sat alert at Misawa and often scrambled to intercept Soviet aircraft as part of the Northern Air Defense Sector, which also included alert JASDF F-15s at Chitose Air Base. For the most part however, any interaction with Soviet or Russian hardware was a result of happenstance and was usually limited to finding empty Russian food cans along the beach at Ripsaw Range. Leave it to Smoky to highlight this to me during the morning range inspection of my range control officer (RCO) checkout!

Many guys were eager to see Ivan first-hand and put a face to all of the intel photos and slides that we were supposed to know. Occasionally, the intel shop would provide coordinates for a Soviet vessel in the area. Depending on the flight lead you would either avoid that particular area (13th FS standard) or troll for the ship with your radar and use his position as bullseye for low-altitude intercepts (14th FS standard!), where the merges, of course, would occur overhead the ship! A Soviet AGI (intelligence gathering ship) would always show up on Day One of our local readiness exercises and park himself three miles off the departure end of runway 10 listening to our radios and telephones. It was difficult to screw with him though, as the SOF in the control tower could monitor your behavior in the traffic pattern. The most the AGI got was afterburner passes on initial or on an "extended" departure leg.

One morning in 1993, Elvis and I were patrolling for ships in the Tsugaru Straits between Hokkaido and Honshu. Elvis directed a ***Maverick*** attack on a radar target 25 miles on our nose. Initial targeting video displayed a surfaced, fast attack submarine heading west. We followed up our simulated missile shots with a BDA pass and determined it was *not* a U.S. sub. We had no clue who it belonged to but it really didn't matter—*it wasn't ours!* We spent twenty minutes "attacking" the sub trying to get "Ivan" to come out of the tube and onto the deck so we could ***ID*** his uniform, but that never happened. Looking at *Jane's Fighting Ships* in the intel shop after the sortie, it did look similar to the Soviet Yankee Class sub, but we never confirmed anything with anybody. In the end, it looked foreign so we'll call it Red because it makes a good story. We did learn that you could pass very low over subs without fear of encountering the multitude of gulls that always hovered over the Russian fishing trawlers!

Engine change at Hakodate Air Base Japan following an emergency landing for an engine problem. (Author)

Aside from the MiG-25 that Viktor Belenko landed at Hakodate in 1976, encountering Soviet aircraft proved rare. Occasionally, a radar contact well over the ocean would be identified as a "stranger" by GCI, and they would later debrief you that your contact was indeed a Soviet Bear or Badger. On 31 August 1993, I was upgrading one of our new guys, KC, on a defensive Air Combat Maneuvering (*ACM*) ride in the C4S area off the west coast of Northern Honshu. We were Fang flight, and JP was number three in the formation. He would be the "bandit" for the ride, with KC and me working on our visual lookout and defensive reactions. Nearing our final engagement, Japanese GCI called our flight on Guard pushing us to a different frequency. The sense of urgency in his voice caught our attention. Headwork (or "Heddowokku" as he struggled to call himself!) gave me a range and bearing to a "no-notice" target. I responded with "Fang, commit 230" and pumped KC to tactical formation. JP immediately called "Bingo" (HUH?) so he RTB'd.

Twenty-five miles from the target, GCI began giving us vectors *away* from the "stranger." I ignored his "suggestions," thinking I could blame it on his poor English if I had to answer later to leadership. I could hear two JASDF F-1s receiving close control for their intercept, which we observed on our radar. We converted on a Soviet IL-20 Coot A, a four-engine electronic combat version of the IL-18 (the P-3ski). The F-1s were flying outrigger by this time and we didn't want to make them too nervous, so we got just close enough to look at the red star on the vertical stabilizer and followed him north for a bit. The Pacific Stars & Stripes reported the intercept the following day, highlighting the fact that it had been a year since the last Soviet airspace violation.

I wonder how the Coot debrief went back at Korsakov! *Japanese* GCI gives blind warnings in *Russian* and "bogey dope" (our vectors to the intercept) in *English*, and the USAF F-16s respond to GCI in *Japanese*! Both KC and I had taken Japanese at *the Zoo* and we found that when the controllers were being difficult, you could almost always get what you wanted by speaking to them in Japanese.

Dano in the squadron flagship over Alaska. (Author)

Perhaps most confusing to the Soviet Intel folks who reviewed the radar tapes of C4S would be why Fang 3 (JP), who was the dedicated *offensive* ACM bandit and the only one with radar, was always getting gunned unobserved from Fang 1 and 2! The only viable tactic we may have compromised that day was sneaking up behind JP in the non-radiate mode of the radar and then turning it on to force JP to immediately break into a gun shot. After all, it was all the holes in his wings that led him to Bingo-out so early![2]

The third pilot I had the chance to interview would probably be considered a "third generation" Samurai, with the initial cadre being the first and pilots like Sluggo and Dano being second. He spent four years with the Samurai and saw two different versions of the Viper, the Block 30 and the Block 50.

Smokin'

I arrived at Misawa to join the 14th in June, 1991. I started my Air Force career at the Air Force Academy, graduating in 1989. After a year of pilot training at Sheppard AFB, TX, I attended Lead-In Fighter Training (LIFT) at Holloman AFB, NM. Following this, I spent six months suffering at the RTU for F-16s at MacDill AFB, Florida. I was officially blessed as a qualified, if not mission ready, F-16 pilot in June of 1991 and reported to Misawa that month. I was finally certified as mission ready in September of that same year. If you're doing the math, that is two years from starting pilot training to being mission ready! I saw the transition to the Block 50 before departing the 14th in 1995.

The training at Holloman lasted about three months and was spent in the AT-38B. The biggest difference between this and the regular T-38 was the paint job, but each jet did have a gunsight in the front cockpit and it could carry a centerline-mounted gun pod or bomb rack. It was at LIFT that we were introduced to the fundamentals of the bombing pattern, air-to-ground gunnery, and the rudiments of Basic Fighter Maneuvers (***BFM***, one versus one combat), Air Combat Maneuvering (ACM, two versus one) and Air Combat Tactics (***ACT***, two or more versus two or more). The training there was fun, but in a lot of ways it was like trying to drink water from a firehose. There was a ton of information for a pilot to absorb in three months. Most of my time there is remembered as a blur, with the air-to-ground training seeming much more concrete. The mechanics of dropping a bomb, for some reason, seemed easier to comprehend.

AT-38 on the flightline at Holloman AFB NM. (Author)

I arrived at MacDill AFB, Florida in November 1990. We spent the first month or so of RTU doing nothing but learning systems and flying the simulator. With today's fighters, transitioning from one to the other is mostly about learning new systems and procedures. The flying is pretty much taken for granted, with none of these airplanes having any special areas where the pilot has to watch out. For example, I remember we spent an entire day learning how to change radio channels, *IFF* codes, and inserting navigation points into the INS! The designers have made it so that when in the thick of combat, you don't have to think about the flying. The hard part is employing the airplane. Since you're not worried about constantly departing the jet (putting it out of control), you can worry about all sorts of other things!

Starting out with the design of the cockpit, it is obvious that a lot of thought and human-factors engineering went into the Viper. You sit fairly high in the cockpit, with the canopy rails just above your elbows. The canopy is on "backwards", eliminating the canopy bow. This means you don't have a place to hang a mirror, but who needs one when you can turn around and see the rudder?

Smokin' starting engines at Cope Thunder. (Jane Thole)

There is nothing in front of you to block your view forward, with the Head Up Display (HUD) being the only thing out there. You can't even see the nose of the airplane. The seat is reclined 30 degrees and makes for a very comfortable and natural seating position.

The stick is mounted on the right side of the cockpit, and of course it's covered in switches and buttons, nine to be exact. The throttle is a goofy shaped contraption and has six buttons and switches of its own. The throttle is just about form fit to your hand though and it is very easy to make the switches do what you want them to, using mainly your thumb and index finger. Almost all of the switches are multifunction, some being five-way switches. That is, they move up, down, left, right, and you can push them in.

Probably the final thing you'll notice about the cockpit is the large keypad sitting right in front of you, just below the HUD. This is called the Up Front Controls, or UFC. On this handy gadget you can do just about anything you would need to do in flight. Change radio channels, change IFF codes, insert nav points into the INS, set the radar altimeter, set up the *ILS* frequency and course for the flight director, and on and on and on. If you ever do need to take your hand off of the throttle in flight, chances are you will be messing with the UFC. This means that the side panels in the jet, although full of switches, are rarely used in flight. You will do a lot of work with them after you start up and before you taxi but probably not once you have taken the runway. About the only task you have to do in-flight on the side panels is turn on the camera.

What makes the Viper such a superb single seat fighter are the systems in the airplane. You no longer need to devote quite so much time to a single task like navigation or searching with the radar so you can do both simultaneously. The Viper has a standard complement of navigation aids, such as TACAN and ILS. The heart of the system, though, is the INS. [3]

This was a good chance to ask Smokin' how some of this compared to the RF-4s that the 14th had previously. I asked him to be as detailed as he could, as I thought it would be the kind of thing that the older generation of 14th pilots would be interested in. He explained how the Viper is set up.

> Instead of the 4 NM per hour drift rate of the RF-4 that Amos Parker mentioned, the INS in the Viper will typically not be more than a half mile off after a sortie, and that is with no updates. If the INS was ever off by more than a mile, then that was reason to have it looked at. Now that the Block 40 and 50 have the Global Positioning Systems (**GPS**), the Viper is even more accurate.
>
> We spent a good deal of time and sorties at pilot training and LIFT learning how to navigate at low-level and at a fairly high speed. Cross-checking the ground with your stopwatch and the map was very time-consuming and for me, stressful. With the INS, though, navigation has become almost a lost art. We still compute time, distance, and heading to each turnpoint along a route of flight, but we don't need to constantly monitor our position. As we approach the turnpoint, we check what the INS says the time/distance/heading to the next point is, and if it agrees with what we planned, we simply follow the steering provided in the HUD to the next point. We do still carry maps, although not strictly for navigation. We use them more to identify where we are in relation to AAA or SAMS and to aid in target acquisition.[4]

One of the primary reasons that the F-4 had two seats was that with the technology of the time, it simply wasn't possible for one man to run the radar, navigate to the target at over 500 knots at low level, and still check six for bad guys. It sounds like some major strides in navigation have been made. What about the radar?

I've had a chance to see the displays from an F-4, and the Viper's radar display would probably make all of the TRS WSOs drool! There is absolutely no clutter on the scope from ground returns. As for range capability, suffice it to say that the Viper can see farther than it has the capability to shoot. We can't see as far as an Eagle, but we see far enough.

The air-to-ground radar modes are equally impressive. We have the standard ground map modes, plus more processing to provide a map with a 64:1 improvement in resolution over the ground map picture. This is not as good as the F-15E or the B-1, but it is very easy to pick out runway intersections, small bridges, fencelines, and the like.

Because of the heavy overcasts in Northern Japan, we practiced dropping bombs through the weather quite a bit. As most of the targets may be radar "no shows," offset aiming is the norm. That is, we find a point near the target that we *can* see on the radar and then input the bearing and range from this offset aimpoint (OAP) into the INS. Once airborne, we find this OAP on the radar and put the radar cursors over it. The jet can now do the math to display where the real target is and figure out a bombing solution. Radar interpretation was a skill that took many pilots a year or two to master. I can't tell you how many times I have been unable to break out the point on the radar only to be able to see it plain as day on the tape during the debrief. It just takes time to see the picture.[5]

At the point that I interviewed Smokin', he had about 1,600 hours in the Viper. He had mentioned earlier that the flying was almost taken for granted and the hard part was employing the airplane. I asked him some questions about the Viper's flying qualities.

The F-16 is, without a doubt, the easiest airplane to fly that I have ever come across. This is after spending a year in the T-37 and T-38, hundreds of hours in various types of gliders, and 200 or so hours in various general aviation airplanes. Compared to the T-38, the Viper is almost boring to take cross-country. The T-38 had no autopilot and was very sensitive in both pitch and roll. A second's inattention would find you 300 feet off of your assigned altitude and listening to Air Traffic Control yell at you for not being where you were supposed to be. This sensitivity made the airplane a lot of fun to fly, as long as you kept your speed up.

Putting the T-38 through its paces in the traffic pattern, though, was always very stressful for me. It seemed that the majority of pilot trainees fit into one of two categories, those that had trouble with the turn to final, and those who had trouble flaring the airplane to touch down. I was one of the guys that always sweated the final turn, but was able to land smoothly.

The T-38 was designed during the 1950s and was made to go fast. That meant that its slow speed qualities were not what you would call ideal. While this made for a superb training platform, it was not worry free. In order to keep the airplane somewhat close to the runway on downwind, the final turn was flown on the ragged edge between flight and a stall. At least it seemed like it to me at the time. The instructors at Sheppard took every chance they could to point out that the majority of fatalities in the T-38 were in the final turn. The airplane was great in that it did give you plenty of warning prior to the stall, with the wings buffeting and eventually starting to rock if you pulled too far. The problem was, you flew the entire pattern in the buffet and it can be difficult to always distinguish the moderate buffet that meant optimum performance from the heavy buffet which immediately preceded a stall. The T-38, post stall, would not spin but would fall like a rock, with the wings mostly level and the nose staying where you put it. This meant that you had to make very accurate judgements as to the wind and the effect it had on your landing pattern. You just did not have the luxury of increasing bank angle and back stick if you found yourself overshooting final! Plus, most of the pilot training bases had two parallel runways, one for the T-38s and one for the T-37s. You couldn't overshoot by much without barging in on the Tweets. And of course, since we were all budding fighter pilots we would not be caught dead flying a wide "bomber pattern"!

Luckily, my class did not have any fatalities during pilot training. The only time we came close was when one of the students was practicing a no-flap approach in the T-38. This put the T-38 in a very nose-high attitude on final, blocking out a good portion of the runway ahead from view. Another student, in a T-37, was on the ground and crossing the runway approach end at the same time with his canopy open. The T-38s main gear went right through the raised canopy of that Tweet, to the surprise of both sets of pilots! No one was hurt, thank God. Both students got a great lesson on clearing the runway before you land or cross. I guess my only point about all that was that the F-16 doesn't really have any area where you have to be especially mindful, like the T-38 in the final turn.

With a full load of fuel and bombs on a hot day, the takeoff distance is rarely over half of the runway length and a lightly loaded, clean (meaning no external stores) Viper can get on the ground and stopped inside of half a runway length. After a typical mission, though, with bomb racks and tanks still hanging, you could still get it stopped well short of the departure end and not need a drag chute or to really stomp on the brakes. Typical rotation speed is around 150 knots and final is flown in that same ballpark, with touchdown being around 140 or 130 knots. Because of the way that the flight controls are set up, the jet does not fly itself off of the runway. It would be content to scream down the runway at 400 knots if you didn't pull it off of the ground!

Landings are a piece of cake to set up, though it is tough to grease one on. We get a lot of lift even at slow speed and if you try to hold the jet off the runway for a "greaser" you can float for a long time! This made landings fun at Paya Lebar airport in Singapore, where we deployed once or twice a year to fly against the Singapore Air Force and to show the flag in the region. The runway there was flat for the first 800 feet or so, then dipped down for the next 2,000 or 3,000 feet. Fighter pilots always try to touchdown somewhere between 500 and 1,000 feet from the approach end of the runway. We would sit outside the operations building every time a flight came back to land to watch the show. If you didn't put the jet down in the first 800 feet, you were not going to touch runway until you were at least 3,000 feet down! We always had a contest to see who would land the longest and the winner, of course, owed everyone beer.[6]

Probably every book ever written about the Viper has mentioned the flight controls. The fly-by-wire controls are still a marvel to everyone familiar with aviation and are just now becoming common to fighter design. While I didn't want Smokin' to cover old ground, I did want to hear from someone who flies the airplane every day to see if he had any additional insights over the "pilot reports" written by magazine editors and professional authors. So, in order to keep the trend alive, I asked about the flight controls!

> The airplane was designed to be unstable in certain regimes and this makes for a very maneuverable airplane. This also means that it could potentially be a handful to fly. Lockheed used the fly-by-wire system to solve this problem and also to save some weight. You see, in all previous airplanes, the control stick in the cockpit was connected directly to the flight controls, either through cables and pulleys or with a hydraulic line, similar to a car's power steering. So, when you move the stick, the flight controls follow. In the Viper, the stick is not connected to the controls! Rather, it is connected to a series of flight control computers, which in turn send electrical signals to flight control actuators. When I push on the stick (it only moves about a quarter inch in each direction), I am asking for a specific response from the jet and the computers make the controls move whatever amount is necessary to make that happen. Sensors in the stick record how hard I push and that drives the amount of response.
>
> Since a computer is actually moving the controls, the engineers were able to make the airplane fly in any way they saw fit, even if it means that the airplane doesn't always behave like an airplane! Take the trim system, for example. You rarely need to trim in the Viper. The only time is if you have asymmetric stores loaded, such as a bomb on only one side. Then you might need to put in a bit of rudder or aileron trim.

In a conventional airplane, you trim for airspeed. Well, technically, you trim for an angle of attack but in level flight it's easier to think in terms of airspeed. Anyway, you zero out the control forces at a certain airspeed. Then, when you reduce power, the airplane will nose over in an attempt to maintain that airspeed. Same for a power increase, where the nose will rise. In the F-16, you trim for G. With neutral trim set, the airplane will attempt to maintain 1 G. So, if you are stabilized in level flight at 150 knots and subsequently light the AB, accelerating to 600 knots, no trim changes are required. The down side to this is that you do not get a "seat of the pants" feel for increasing or decreasing airspeed through the stick. This is easily overcome by looking at your airspeed in the HUD! Other airplanes have taken different routes. The Hornet, for example, has a trim system setup just like the Viper but only when the gear is up. When the landing gear is down, it behaves just like a normal airplane with respect to trim and airspeed. This is why the Hornet will fly itself off of the runway and the Viper won't.[7]

One of the most controversial topics of conversation concerning the Viper is the flight control limiters. These limiters are control laws, written into the flight control computer, to keep you from going out of control or over G-ing the jet. People who don't know any better complain, "I don't want a computer flying the airplane for me! When I want to do something, I don't want some stupid computer telling me I can't!" If the flight control laws are written correctly though, they enhance your performance, not limit it. In the F-16, they are written correctly!

I've read that in the F-4, when the angle of attack (AOA, the angle between the wing and the relative airflow) increases, you had better not think of moving the stick to roll the aircraft. Rudder is how you do it. Not so in the F-16. At all airspeeds and AOA, if you want roll, you push the stick sideways. If you want yaw, you hit the rudder. When you push sideways on the stick, the jet knows you are asking for roll and will move the control surfaces in the proper combination to give you what you asked for, even if this means deflecting the rudder to make the jet roll.

At high airspeed, the jet is limited to nine Gs. As you get slower, the computer takes AOA into account and will not let you go past an AOA which would cause the wings to stall and the aircraft to go out of control. What this means is that when you want a maximum performance turn, you pull back on the stick, hard, and you can be assured that the jet is giving you everything it can without over G-ing or going out of control.

It is common to come back from fighting Eagles or Hornets and hear them raving about the turn performance of the Viper. This isn't because the Viper is aerodynamically superior to the F-15 or F-18. Superior in just about every other way, but not always aerodynamically! But, we can take full advantage of our turn capability whereas an Eagle pilot is constantly worried about departing or over G-ing his aircraft. Well, that may not be fair. The Eagle is easier to maneuver than the F-4, but still not as carefree as the Viper. Either way, since it takes almost perfect pilot technique to get the most out of their airplane, it is uncommon to see them actually get it.

Does this mean you can't depart the Viper? Hardly. Every year two or three Vipers get put out of control, and sometimes the pilot can't recover and has to eject. The thing that makes the Viper such a great airplane (and the characteristic that silences the critics) is that for all practical purposes the limiters don't come into play until *after* you've made a control input. When I pull full aft on the stick, the horizontal tails deflect fully. Immediately afterward though, the computer starts to analyze AOA, airspeed, yaw rate, and a host of other variables to see if that was such a good idea. If the control inputs I just made are driving the jet past an AOA limit, the control surfaces will automatically move to correct the situation. If you are too slow (in terms of airspeed and intelligence!) then the controls do not have the aerodynamic authority to override your input, and out of control you go. In other words, you asked for it and you got it. You still need to have a great degree of finesse to fly the airplane to the edge of its envelope.

When the F-16 departs, it usually doesn't spin. It will normally just fall like a rock while staying fairly level. Once the computers sense that you are out of control, you are locked out of the control loop and the controls automatically try to recover the airplane. If they don't, then we have a way in the cockpit to override the override, if you will, and recover the airplane.[8]

At this point, I had to ask Smokin' if he'd ever put a Viper out of control!

Yeah, my brush with fame came on my first unsupervised ride after we had converted to Block 50s. I had about 900 hours in the Block 30 at this point, I was an instructor pilot (IP), and I was feeling pretty confident. O.K., maybe cocky, but confident sounds better! The Block 50 is a bit heavier than the Block 30 and because of this, the jet is a little more sluggish in pitch. I was flying out over the west coast of Northern Japan, in what we called the Charlie airspace. I was flying BFM and my wingman, "Mule," had started out on the offense. I pulled the nose up in an effort to get him to spit out front. I had the nose of the aircraft about 45 degrees high, and the airspeed around 110 KIAS. He had enough airspeed and range back from me to pull his nose up as well and try to take a gunshot. I jammed the stick back and to the left to start defending and to try to overshoot him. I had done this dozens of times in the Block 30 with no problems. In the Block 50, the heavy nose made this maneuver exceed the AOA and yaw limits. The nose started to move down and to the left as requested, then stopped and rapidly reversed to the right, yawing 270 degrees to put me upside down! The jet was too slow to self-recover and I started to fall like a rock. I was wings level, inverted, and the nose was bobbing up and down in relation to the horizon. Hanging in the straps, I had to reach forward and "down" for the MPO switch. Pushing on the MPO, I then had to push full forward on the stick to get the nose tracking up in relation to the horizon. The nose went up about 15 degrees or so, then started to move back down. As soon as it did, I pulled full aft on the stick to get the nose down and try to break the stall. Luckily, the nose continued to track downward and when it was about 45 degrees nose low, inverted, the jet shuddered and continued tracking. I now had to push full forward to stop the nose rate with the nose pointing straight down to pick up airspeed. Then it was a matter of releasing the MPO switch and recovering from the dive. This whole time Mule had been watching my imitation of a falling leaf, and my actual performance as an idiot, calling out altitude on the radio. At the time the TRs stated that if you were out of control below 10,000 feet AGL you were to eject. I was technically still out of control passing 10,000 but the nose was moving downward at that point and I knew I had it made. I had the privilege of spending an hour or so with the squadron commander, "GAK," discussing the finer points of not being a ham-fist with the jet when it is slow! He's a great guy and he reasoned that if you don't put a jet out of control at some point in your career then you're not really performing to the maximum of your abilities, or those of the jet. He promptly scheduled me for a BFM ride against him the next day so I could get back on the horse that threw me. [9]

Aside from the brief time flying P-51s in WW II, the 14th has never been able to strike back at the enemy, empty fuel tanks and toilet paper notwithstanding! I asked Smokin' about the missions the 14th trained for.

>The mission we trained for the most was interdiction, flying as part of a strike package to attack some strategically important target. A typical loadout would be two external tanks of fuel, two *AIM-120* AMRAAM radar guided missiles, two AIM-9 *Sidewinder* infrared (IR) guided missiles, and whatever bombs were necessary to destroy the target. The two tanks take up two external stations, leaving us with three others that could carry bombs. The center station was usually loaded with some sort of Electronic Countermeasures (ECM) pod so our typical load would be two 2,000 pound bombs, six 500 pounders, or four cluster bomb units.
>
>Northern Japan was a great place to fly. There was often pretty thick cloud cover over land, but the visibility was

always great and you weren't hampered by the silly rules the FAA imposes on us here in the States. With all of the mountains, the flying at low level was a lot of fun when the cloud cover was high enough.

Smokin' on a training sortie west of Misawa. (Author)

In fact, I was flying one day and we could see our target from 160 miles away! We were flying as a package of 12 F-16s, led by one of our IPs named Slam. As we were marshalling in the northern part of the our airspace, I glanced to the south toward our target to get a feel for the weather. We were simulating an attack on a port facility on an island off of the west coast of Japan. I saw an island down there that looked like the target photos we had studied an hour earlier during the briefing. Could that be the target? Sure enough, next time around in the CAP and the steerpoint symbol in the HUD was sitting right on that island!

I've seen visibility to rival that since in Alaska but haven't been able to see a target from that far away.

There was a bombing range ten miles north of Misawa, called Ripsaw, where we could drop practice bombs and inert munitions. For tactical training, we had plenty of realistic targets to train with. Low altitude attacks were normally flown against coastal targets. This allowed us to make part of our attack run over water, cutting down on the noise complaints. Plus, the mountainous terrain in the area, combined with the almost ever-present cloud cover, meant that coastal targets were sometimes the only ones with weather good enough for a low altitude attack, as long as you made your run-in over water.

In a typical low altitude attack, a flight of four Vipers would approach the target at 500 feet, doing 540 knots or greater. Between four and five miles from the target, we would make a four to five G check turn away from the target, delay for a few seconds, then make a four to five G pull up into a steep climb. We made that check turn so that in the climb, we would be able to search for the target without the nose of the airplane getting in the way. Once we spotted the target, we would again use four to five Gs to roll toward the target, lining up the bombsight symbology in the HUD with the target. After releasing the weapon for the day, a five to six G escape maneuver was in order to get back to low altitude, avoid the explosion from our own bombs, and to avoid any target area threats.

Medium altitude attacks were made on just about anything we could find, as the noise wasn't a factor. Well, sometimes it wasn't a factor. One of the pilots in the 13th earned his nickname "Mach" for laying a sonic boom over one of the nearby towns during an attack, causing a lot of broken windows and phone calls to the wing commander! We had an outstanding target intel shop at the Wing and they produced a set of books with photos and coordinates for thousands of different targets in the area.

With the change to the Block 50, the emphasis has shifted slightly away from interdiction and toward SEAD and air-to-air. The mission the 14th is usually assigned is termed "Force Protection." SEAD typically is limited to surface-to-air threats but with the awesome air-to-air capabilities of the Viper they will often take the place of the F-15s in the strike package, escorting the strikers into the target area and then killing SAMs before they can shoot back.

To do this, the Block 50 is equipped with the HARM Targeting System (HTS) pod. It is roughly shaped like an oversized football and is mounted on the right side of the engine inlet. It is capable of locating and identifying SAM radars. The pilot then decides which SAMs are going to be a factor to the strikers. The HARM guides on the radar emissions of the target and takes out the site, leaving the area clear for the strikers. The pilot has to combine his knowledge of the strike routing, the enemy forces strength and location, and timing to determine when and at which site to launch. Often, he will be defending against the SAM himself.

The HTS pod does some good work. When a signal is received, it is identified and displayed along the edge of the pilot's Multi-Function Display (MFD) to show what azimuth it is coming from. When the site is located, it is displayed on the MFD and the pilot can see the latitude, longitude, and other parameters of the site.

You hear a lot of old Weasel pilots bad mouth the Viper as a SEAD asset, but to be honest, that is because they simply don't know any better. It's the same thing you hear when a bunch of ex-F-111 drivers get together and start badmouthing the F-15E. In the Mudhen's case, the 15E maybe can't go as far and as fast as the 'Vark down low, but when you combine the accuracy of the Mudhen's weaponry with its air-to-air capability, there is no comparison. Same for the Viper versus the F-4G. We had a few ex-Phantom Weasel pilots in our squadron, and they were all happy with the capabilities of the Viper and the HTS pod. That was in '95, and the jet and pod have been through two major upgrades since then.

Because of our coastal location we got to execute a mission unique to Misawa, maritime attack. Maritime attack was something not to be taken lightly. Anyone who has studied naval operations knows that a battle group can be very formidable. With the ocean being so flat, the boats will usually know you are there well before you can spot them. Since there was an entire carrier battle group stationed in Tokyo, we had many opportunities to practice. If we couldn't find a naval vessel, the coastline had plenty of freighters making their way north and south to practice on. The only way we had a chance against a heavily defended ship was to team up with the Navy P-3s that were also stationed at Misawa. The P-3 is a large, four-engined beast loaded with torpedoes, Harpoon anti-ship missiles, and depth charges. We did a lot of coordination with the Navy to come up with a system where they would find and identify the boats and then we would team up to attack them. We'd simulate launching whatever weapons we could, hoping to stay out of range of their defenses. The theory was, if we then spotted smoke rising from the target, the rest of the Vipers could attack with Mavericks or bombs. The Maverick is an excellent anti-ship weapon, and we practiced this often.

A lot of the Maverick attacks we did were from low altitude. Because you spend a lot of time looking inside the cockpit trying to lock the Maverick seeker on the target, you didn't want your new wingman flying into a mountain while he was still learning the system. So, we would normally train guys by attacking boats off of the coast before we went after targets over land. The radar had no trouble locking on to the ships, thus they were easy to find at long range. This gave you plenty of time to set up your attack without worrying about terrain. Plus, the boats were usually easy to see, both with the eye and through the Maverick seeker. It takes some time to learn how to interpret the picture presented on the MFD by the Maverick seeker, but a hot ship on a cold ocean was a very easy target to identify, thus making it perfect for a new guy or an old guy who is out of practice. I don't know if the boats' crews appreciated our repeated low passes but I sure enjoyed them! After almost every sortie like that the crew chief would have to wash down the plane to clean off the salt spray!

One of the neatest things about flying at Misawa was the chance to fight a variety of different airplanes and pilots from different countries. Besides U.S. F-15s and Navy/Marine F-14s, F/A-18s, and AV-8B Harriers, I had a chance to fight Japanese F-4s, RF-4s, F-15s, and F-1s. Trips to Malaysia, Thailand, South Korea, and Singapore added F-5s, A-4s, and F-16As to my list of opponents.

Stationed with us at Misawa were two squadrons of Mitsubishi F-1s, a ground attack airplane very similar in appearance and performance to the British Jaguar. It has a basic air-to-ground radar and was used for maritime attack by the JASDF. We did not fight these guys often as it was a bit of a mismatch. More often, we would include them in our strike packages to practice coordination and work on our interoperability.

Mitsubishi F-1 at the Misawa Airshow, summer 1991. (Author)

I got a chance to fly the F-1 simulator once when I diverted to Matsushima Air Base, 137 NM south of Misawa. Six of us ended up there because of bad weather at Misawa. Two of our airplanes broke while there, giving me and "Hotrod" the opportunity to spend the week. Matsushima was the Japanese equivalent of Holloman, providing training to new fighter pilots before they were assigned to their units. They had a few simulators there and invited Hotrod and me to try our hand at the mighty F-1. I was surprised to find it very similar to the T-38, both in terms of the cockpit and the flying qualities. There was a radar screen buried at the bottom of the instrument panel and dials everywhere. There was no HUD to speak of, just a gunsight which had a reticle and a projection of a compass on it. The F-1 was very sensitive in pitch and roll, having a tremendous roll rate. Pull on the stick, though, and the plane would shake and shudder, telling you that you weren't going to win a turning fight in this airplane. We would often get to watch these guys in the bombing and strafing pattern at Ripsaw. They could drop a pretty good bomb, considering that it was a completely manual system.

For some reason, the Japanese felt it necessary to show all of their pilots just what vertigo felt like. One of their simulators was set up to do just that. Kind of like practicing bleeding if you ask me. It was a standard F-1 simulator, but the visual screen was mounted on the left side. You would get in and try to fly formation on another F-1, projected on that screen. You would start out on a nice sunny day, with the flight lead doing a series of right and left turns. Then, they would take away the sky/ground projection and replace it with a gray background, just like you were in the weather. After working up a sweat at this, they replaced the "weather" with a random, fluctuating striped pattern. Really bizarre and hard to hang on to! As if that wasn't enough, they would then spin the simulator, just to make sure you were really messed up! Hotrod and I both got out of this sim a little shaky and glad that the USAF didn't buy this contraption!

The Japanese F-4s were a bit tougher to fight than the F-1s. Most of them still had the older APQ-120 radars, although they were being upgraded with F-16 radars as I left. Beyond Visual Range (BVR), they were as tough to fight as anybody else, having the capability to find you and shoot you BVR. It was possible to defeat these older radars, however, and the fights usually progressed to the visual merge. In this type of fight, the F-4 was totally outmatched by the Viper. We could turn much tighter, had more thrust, and had much better visibility. But, just like fighting any other adversary, if the Phantoms made fewer mistakes than you did it was going to be a tough day for you, no matter what you were flying.

JASDF F-4EJ at Gifu Air Base, Japan. (Author)

In the summer of 1992, we were on a two-week deployment to Kadena Air Base, on the island of Okinawa. We deployed there to get away from the sea fog that covered Misawa during the summer months, sometimes shutting down flying for a week at a time. Many times I remember being in the instrument pattern, at 1,500 feet AGL, with all of the clouds *below* me!

The deployment sortie down there was a doozie for a first lieutenant with 250 hours in the jet. I was still a wingman and was flying on the wing of my Flight Commander, a Fighter Weapons School graduate by the name of "Taboo." We were carrying 4 Mk. 20 Rockeye apiece, a cluster munition designed to kill tanks. The Rockeye had been declared obsolete by the Air Force and we were dropping it basically to get rid of the stuff. I was part of an eight-ship strike package attacking a target on an island north of Okinawa, defended by eight F-15s from Kadena. The flight from Misawa was about two hours, all spent at 25,000-30,000 feet and requiring us to refuel from a KC-135 prior to the fight. We were going to ingress initially at this altitude, dropping to the deck in an attempt to get past the F-15s and attack them from below on our way to the target. As we made contact with the Eagles on our radar, we waited to get to the appropriate range when Taboo radioed, "Shack, take it down!" We all rolled inverted and pulled into a steep dive, pulling out 500 feet over the Pacific. Having flown at 30,000 feet for the past two and a half hours, my canopy was very cold. Combine this with the high humidity at low altitude and you get condensation, a lot of it! As soon as we rolled out at low altitude, Taboo started to disappear and I couldn't see the water anymore. I first thought I had flown into a cloud, but that was impossible, as there weren't any! Instead, a cloud had flown into me! I spent the next few minutes roasting in the cockpit and wiping frantically at the canopy to regain sight of lead! I had to turn the heater and canopy defrost on full blast to clear the ice on the inside of the canopy! Luckily, we made it to the target, I dropped my bombs on the island (I won't say I hit the target, but I did hit the island!), and we made it into Kadena unscathed.

The one time I had a chance to fight RF-4s was a real eye-opener. It might seem to be a mismatch to have F-16s fighting RF-4s, but that really wasn't the case. This was before the F-16 was carrying AMRAAMs, so all we had was short range Sidewinders. We paired off, two Vipers against two JASDF Reccies. We were defending one side of the airspace and the Reccie's job was to get past us to their target. Our tactic was to find the RF-4s and attack them from low to high, giving our missile a nice blue background and making it difficult for the RFs to find us. The Reccie's tactic was simple. Use the jamming pod, fly high and fly fast, then when the GCI controller says the Vipers are close, start putting out a ton of flares to try decoying the AIM-9. You've heard already how fast the RF is, and I can attest to that fact. Attacking a high, fast flyer with IR missiles takes perfect technique and a lot of speed. We would sometimes find ourselves stuck at six o'clock, outside of range to shoot. If we did manage the intercept right, we still had to wait for the RF to stop puking out flares before we could shoot. The problem was more difficult than any of us had imagined. My flight lead, "Ice", had flown F-4s so I imagine it was interesting for him to see things from the other side. Most of our other missions there were flown either against the USAF Eagles or the JASDF F-4s. We were all relieved to get back to fighting these "normal" fighters!

The JASDF also had a squadron of F-15s stationed at Chitose Air Base, a large airfield 126 NM north of Misawa on the island of Hokkaido, near the city of Sapporo. All of us enjoyed it when we got the chance to fight these guys, as it gave us a break from fighting ourselves. The planes they had were fine, but they didn't fly them very hard. Without exception, all of the Japanese pilots I met were superb flyers, able to fly precisely and well. This precision unfortunately made its way into their tactical flying. All of them flew very conservatively, preferring to keep their wingman close to lead at all times. We always joked that you could never take a gunshot on a Japanese fighter because his wingman was always stuck at six o'clock, giving you nowhere to go! But all of the Japanese fighter pilots where just like all of us, eager to learn and loving to fly.

One area in which the JASDF pilots did excel was in intelligence gathering! For the first year or so that I was at Misawa, the AMRAAM missile had not been introduced to the Viper fleet. Subsequently, when we did start flying and training with it everyone was interested, especially our "hosts". An even bigger concern was our proximity to the former Soviet Union. We were convinced, being paranoid fighter pilots during the Cold War, that anybody and everybody was listening to and watching us train. Along with the F-1s and U.S. Navy P-3s I mentioned earlier, the Japanese had a squadron of E-2C Hawkeyes at Misawa. These are the same birds our Navy uses as a shipboard AWACS. Because this was a JASDF airfield and they ran the control tower, they had a copy of our flying schedule everyday. Whenever we launched a four-ship on an air-to-air training sortie, one of their Hawkeyes would take off about an hour earlier and orbit to the west of our airspace. We guessed, rightly or wrongly, that they were recording the fight and our comm so they could analyze it and study our tactics and the capabilities of the AMRAAM.

Consequently, we tried to limit the things we said on the radio. We also limited our tactics whenever we fought them, placing ourselves under strict Visual Identification (VID) rules for the fight. That is, we set up the training scenario such that we had to get close enough to the adversaries to visually identify them as enemy before we could shoot. This prevented us from taking long-range shots and potentially compromising the capabilities of our planes and missiles. We never told the Japanese this though, so they always flew as if we could shoot them from long range. This situation, with us being VID and the Eagles being BVR could have caused us a lot of problems. But, the JASDF was so conservative they made it easy for us.

My checkout as an Instructor Pilot was a case in point. After two years of haggling, we had finally convinced the JASDF that it really was safe to send up a four-ship of their Eagles to oppose a four-ship of our Vipers. Typically, when training in the air-to-air arena, one side is designated as the blue side, or good guys, and the other flight is red, designated training aids. The red flight tries to replicate some threat system, in those days usually that of the Soviet Union. In this case, we let them use all of their systems and missiles full-up, as the AIM-7 Sparrows they carried were excellent substitutes for the Soviet AA-7 carried by the Flogger and the AA-10 carried by the Fulcrum. We told them we would be carrying AMRAAMs and AIM-9s, but didn't tell them our ID criteria.

We fought off of the west coast, with the JASDF doing a fighter sweep against us in the south. They gave us two groups of two Eagles each, with the two groups separated in azimuth by about 15 miles. We detected them, I directed my number three to target the eastern group, and we pushed north, preparing to execute a tactic to confuse them and get them to drop us from their radar. Well, to our surprise, at about 25 NM, all four of them turned around and ran north! To hell with our tactic, we'll just keep pressing them north and see what they do! After about a minute, they all turned back south toward us and the adrenaline again began to flow. Soon our Radar Warning Receivers (RWR) began to light up, telling us that they were probably launching AIM-7s at us. As we began to defend, they all turned and ran again! So much for our missile defense! At this point, we were about seven to eight miles behind them and able to see them with our eyeballs for the first time. I cleared my number three off to engage the eastern group and all four of us plugged in the AB to get close enough to VID these guys. Three and four were split off to the east, so it was just my instructor pilot, "Pigpen," and me against the western group. At this point, all we could see were two dots in front of us. Granted, they were big dots, since they were Eagles, but still just dots nonetheless. We were just waiting for them to turn so we could ID them. The two Eagles were flying a line-abreast formation, and they picked this time to do a cross turn right in front of us! That is, the guy on the left turned right and the guy on the right turned left, both back into us. I called, "Fang 2, switch!. ID bandit," as we each picked up the Eagle on the other side of the formation from us. It was painfully easy to shoot them with a simulated AIM-9. The comm we were hearing told us that things had played out basically the same in the east. Needless to say, after one more engagement like that I passed the ride with no problems! The comment Pigpen made on my grade sheet after the ride was, "Excellent results versus not so difficult bandits- no losses." Pretty much sums it up![10]

With all of the TDYs he mentioned, I wanted to ask Smokin' which was his favorite and why.

> We had a ton of great deployments when I was there. In total, I went to Alaska, Thailand, Singapore, Malaysia, South Korea and to five or six different Japanese airbases. One of the best was Thailand. Just about every fighter pilot flying today is a fan, if you will, of the Phantom and Thud drivers who flew during Vietnam. It was a big thrill for us to spend five weeks flying out of Korat and seeing for ourselves the countryside where so much of the USAF's history has been made. The runway and taxiways still have the hills in them that you always see in the film clips, and many of the revetments we parked our jets in were built for the Thuds stationed there years ago. There were a couple of things about that TDY that really stand out in my mind.
>
> The first was the sense of history I mentioned. We all knew the 14th had flown out of Udorn during Vietnam and we wanted to fly by the field and take a look. Sadly, we all didn't have a chance. One of our guys, "Banjo" I think it was, ruined the party for us by making multiple low level, high speed passes over the airfield. He didn't think anything of it and was telling us all about it afterwards when we got the word that it was still an active airfield and the controllers had been frantically trying to tell him so over the radio! Oops.

Pre-takeoff checks at Korat RTAFB, Thailand. (Author)

The second thing about the Thailand deployment was the casual attitude the locals had for safety. One of the main reasons we were there was to practice dropping live weapons. The Thais had designated an area north of the base as a target area. Before we dropped any bombs, we sent a four ship out to scout the area. When "Cow" came back from the sortie, he was a little upset. We went to the Thais and tried to tell them that the area wouldn't work because it was filled with people and their thatch huts. The Thais shrugged their shoulders and said, "Don't worry about it. We told them to move and if they don't, it's their fault." Needless to say, we didn't drop any bombs there.

A day later, one of the A-10s working with us fired a WP rocket at a target and hit a Thai smack in the chest, blowing him to pieces. The A-10 pilot was flying at high altitude and never saw the guy on the range. The Thai had been on the range collecting scrap metal and never heard or saw the attack. When we found out about it, we tried to cancel flying or at least slow down a little to conduct a full investigation. The response of Thais was the same as before. In their opinion, the incident wasn't even worth investigating because the scrap collector had been warned to stay off of the range. Incredible.

Lastly, the TDY pointed out some of the problems you can create for yourself by not training realistically. In training, we rarely carry real bombs and the FACs rarely carry WP rockets. The only way to find the target was to have the FAC describe it for us. We would orbit outside of the target area, far enough away so as not to get shot but close enough to see it. The conversation would sound something like this, with the FAC's callsign being Misty and ours being Shack.

Misty: Shack, confirm you have me in sight?
Shack: Affirmative.
Misty: Off my left wing you will see a large, east-west running river.
Shack: Contact.
Misty: Follow the river east until it makes a 90-degree bend to the south.
Shack: Contact.
Misty: There is a paved road going north-south coming out of that bend. Follow the road north until it makes a "Y."
Shack: Contact.
Misty: Call the distance between the river and the Y one unit. Go one unit east from the "Y" and you will see a circular clearing in the jungle.
Shack: Confirm the clearing has a L shaped lake at the north end.

Misty: Negative. You went too far. This clearing is in a valley, bordered on the west and south by rocky hills.
Shack: Contact.
Misty: Your target is a column of vehicles, parked on the north edge of the clearing.

This takes awhile, and a lot of comm. The problem is even tougher when doing a low altitude attack. Then, you only have 20 seconds or so to ID the target based off of a verbal description and a minute or so of studying a map. In Thailand, it was still difficult but a lot more fun since everyone, the FAC and the fighters, was carrying live weapons. We would get the target description from the FAC, start our run in, and as we were in the pop-up, the FAC would lay down a couple of WP rockets to mark the target. The white smoke stood out great against the green jungle and even if you didn't see the actual trucks in a treeline, the FAC would tell you where to drop in relation to his smoke.

Even an old guy like Cow learned a lesson. I was flying on Cow's wing as number two. We were carrying six 500-pound bombs apiece and would be doing *CAS* with an A-10. We were doing medium altitude attacks and I just couldn't find the target. We must have spent five minutes circling over the target, with Cow trying to talk my eyes onto it, when I actually saw a light bulb appear above his canopy and he came up on the radio and said, "Two, just watch where my bombs hit!" We both felt pretty stupid at that point, but that is the kind of thing that happens when you spend years training without real bombs.[11]

Everyone I interviewed for this book pointed out that the flying at Misawa was some of the best they have ever done. Smokin' echoed these feelings. We got to talking about some of the people he knew while at Misawa, and he wanted to single out one guy in particular.

There were a ton of fine people in the Samurai, too many to mention. One man in particular stands out in my mind though. Not only was he a great guy, but he plays a prominent part in two of the most significant events of my tour. Mark "Mickey" Todd was one of the finest people I have ever met. I say "was" because he was killed a few years ago while on a tour of duty in Central America. He was riding in the back of a Cessna, observing and advising this third-world air force's pilot about something or other, when the pilot he was with crashed, killing all onboard.

Mark "Mickey" Todd. (Author)

Mickey was a tall, quiet guy, but when he did talk it was always worth listening to. He had been an instructor pilot at one of the pilot training bases and this was his first fighter assignment. He was never one of the really "fast burners" of the squadron, but he was so damned levelheaded that he upgraded quickly to flight lead and he had a ton of air sense. I remember two specific incidents that paint a perfect picture of Mickey Todd. I'll tell you about the second one first.

It was the fall of '93. We had taken six jets and deployed to Singapore for four weeks of showing the flag in the South Pacific. The plan was that after one week in Singapore, three jets and six pilots would deploy about an hour's flying time north to Kuantan Air Base, Malaysia and stay there for two weeks. We would spend a week flying air-to-ground missions and then a week of air-to-air with the Malaysian A-4s stationed there. The supervision for the trip was our ops officer "Tootsie," with Mickey being next senior.

The first week went great: the weather was wonderful, the flying good, and all of us got plenty of sun and surf at our beachfront hotel. While the living quarters were nice, the facilities at Kuantan weren't exactly what we were used to. These guys were really a flying club in the truest sense of the word. All of them had been flying their whole career at Kuantan and knew the place inside out. They never flew when the weather was bad and even if they had wanted to, they couldn't have. You see, they were flying ex-U.S. Navy A-4s and as such, they had no ILS installed. They could have flown a GCA in the rain, but when it rained the GCA radar didn't work! Since they never flew the ILS, they didn't even have an approach plate to show us how to fly it.

Believe it or not, one of their older pilots, who remembered what an ILS was, drew the approach for us on a piece of paper and we all made copies. Honest to God, our approach plate was hand drawn. I don't know how Tootsie approved us doing that, but that is another story! He also authorized a contest to see who could enter the traffic pattern the fastest. I think "Flem" was declared the winner at 550 knots on the second day of the contest. We were starting out slow so we could draw out the fun a bit but Tootsie quickly discovered the error of his ways and called the whole thing off before word got out and he got fired. Too bad. I was ready to up the ante to 600 knots!

Well, the second week showed up and so did the seasonal monsoon. For a week straight, it rained harder than I have ever seen before or since. "Luckily" for us, though, the ceiling and visibility would break just about takeoff and land time every day, so pilots and maintainers got a good soaking that week as we worked on the ramp to launch and recover the jets. That Tuesday, Flem and I were first out of the chute. The weather was forecast to be solid clouds from about 1,000 feet to over 30,000 feet, visibility about a mile and a half in pouring rain, and oh-by-the-way, embedded thunderstorms in the clouds. I'm here to tell you, that forecast was good. Speaking of forecasts, the weather shop at Kuantan was also part of the flying club. We came into work one day and glanced at the forecast that the weather shop had sent over. The forecast consisted of one word, "fine"!

Flem and I took off, on a quest to find some clear airspace. Of course, the Malays had cancelled, leaving just us two. I don't think we ever broke out of the weather. I spent the entire time following the vectors the controllers were giving us, my radar set up to search for thunderstorms. Flem was two miles behind me, with his radar locked to me and him just hanging on. We eventually gave up, went back to the field, and shot our hand-drawn approach. The Malay pilot had gotten it right, as the approach worked and brought us right to the ILS without hitting the ground. Since I was in the weather the whole time, I have no idea how close we actually came to any obstacles or terrain, and I don't ever want to find out!

The first thing I did when I got back in the building, after drying off, was to go straight to Tootsie and recommend that we cancel flying for the rest of the day. He went berserk. "Oh my God! I can't believe you guys! When **I** was a lieutenant, I cherished every flying hour I got! I never wanted to cancel a sortie! What's the matter with you guys?" And on and on it went. Mickey was standing in the corner, taking all of this in, smiling to himself. When Tootsie finally came up for air, Mickey just said quietly, "Sir, can I talk to you for a minute?" He motioned for him to follow and he took the ops officer into the adjacent room and closed the door. About ten minutes later, they both came out, and the ops officer announced, "We're canceling flying for the day. It just doesn't make sense given the weather and the instrument facilities here." Mickey probably saved someone's life that day.

The other incident happened a year earlier, in the fall of 1992, when we were deployed to South Korea for a CAS exercise. We were to spend two to three weeks working with the OA-10s of the 25th Fighter Squadron, the Assam Dragons, out of Osan Air Base. We were there to practice working with the 25th and the various U.S. and Korean army units stationed on the peninsula. I had been with the squadron for a little over a year. I was a first lieutenant, had about 300 hours in the jet, and was still a wingman.

This day was a typical Korean winter day. The ground was brown, the sky was gray, and the visibility was about 3 miles in pollution. The weather shop said it was haze, but anybody who went outside and tried to breathe knew better. We were tasked to work with one of the OA-10 FACs and were one of three or four two-ships of fighters working in the Pilsung range complex, about 50 miles east of Osan. When we showed up and checked in, the FAC put us in a holding pattern north of the range while he scouted out the target and coordinated with the ground units. I was flying as number two, on the wing of one of our flight commanders and instructor pilots, Cow. Cow directed me to fighting wing, a formation where I fly in trail of him, maneuvering as required to stay within a couple thousand feet of him and close to his altitude. The altitude was critical, as we were not the only fighters holding at that location. After a few orbits, the FAC found us a target and started to describe it to us. At this point, it's important for the wingman to keep his head outside of the cockpit, as the flight lead is busy plotting coordinates on his map and concentrating solely on the ground, trying to locate the target. I was new to this CAS game, and let myself float high and to the outside of the turn, concentrating too much on the ground picture and not where I was flying. All of a sudden, I hear this deafening "WHOOSH!" and see a dark shape streaking past my canopy, going the opposite direction. Let me tell you, in order to hear another airplane from the cockpit of an F-16, you have to be very close! The canopy is ¾ inches thick, you're wearing a helmet and earplugs, and you get a good bit of noise from your own jet as well. To put it in perspective, even when refueling from a KC-135 or KC-10 and are 15 feet directly underneath one of those behemoths, with their three or four engines right there, you hardly hear a thing.

Smokin's F-16 approaches the boom while on a training sortie at Cope Thunder. Picture was taken from the back seat of a D-model. (Walsh)

I was immediately bathed in a cold sweat as I realized what had happened. I looked behind me and saw a black dot going away. I thought it was the FAC and I had lost track of him. I was able to swallow my fear at almost being dead and continued the mission.

After landing, I was riding back to the squadron in the back of a pickup truck and Mickey hopped in. He had been flying as one of the other sets of fighters on that mission. He just sat there, looking between his feet and nodding as I told him what had happened.

Later that night, we were both sitting at the bar, having a beer and discussing the day's events. I told him how I was scared enough to be thinking about quitting this whole silly game of flying. He let me babble on for about ten minutes or so, and then, in a tone and manner I would become very familiar with in the coming three years, he proceeded to tell me all about how these things happen and that all you can do is prepare yourself as best you can and let God figure out the rest. Now I've summarized, because fighter pilots don't actually talk about things like that in words like those. But even though he was using the words that fighter pilots really use in public, he got the point across.

After a few more beers, and a lot more discussion, we discovered that the dark gray, noisy, fast moving shape had been him, in an orbit that was 1,000 feet higher than I was supposed to be at. He was in a right hand turn, looking to his right, and I was in a left hand turn, looking at the ground. He never saw me and had no idea how close I had come to killing us both. When we figured this out, he just looked at me, smiled, and raised his glass, saying something to the effect of, "Here's to being alive." I wonder what he said to the pilot of that Cessna.[12]

Merge

Merge arrived at Misawa during Smokin's timeframe and he relates a story concerning the 14th's air-to-ground mission. Smokin' mentioned that the flying environment is outstanding at Misawa. In fact, about the only bad thing to be said about the flying at Misawa is that there isn't a decent range close by to drop bombs. Ripsaw range, ten miles to the north of Misawa, is fine for dropping BDU-33s, which are 25 pound practice bombs with a small phosphorous charge for scoring. Inert munitions, concrete filled versions of the standard Mk 82 and Mk 84 (500 and 2000 pound bombs respectively), could be dropped there, but the targets are simply old trucks and airplane parts laid out on the shoreline. This, and the fact that live bombs can't be dropped there at all, makes Ripsaw unsuitable for use as a tactics range. Consequently, the Samurai have to deploy to either Korea or Kadena Air Base on Okinawa to drop heavyweight munitions. Often times, the squadron would marry up these requirements to drop heavyweight bombs with exercises. Such was the case with the next story. Flying fighters, while always a serious business, isn't always serious!

> This story begins at Osan Air Base, Korea in October 1996. The Samurai were deployed to Korea for an exercise known as Foal Eagle 96, or as we called it, Foul Eagle 96. The weather during our time there was Korean standard; it sucked! Very little visibility and clouds up to the moon were the norm.
>
> The particular day in question started with bad weather and it stayed that way all day. The flight was to be led by "Shotgun," I was number two, "Frenchy" was leading the element as number three, and "Gabby" was number four.

The flight was planned to go to Pilsung range to drop MK-84 inerts with a ground FAC controlling us at the range. We were operating out of the west diamond at Osan and we had the jets parked in the hardened shelters there, so we were spread out and had to use a van to get to each jet.

The brief and step all went normally. We lugged all our stuff out and got in the step van to go to the jets. Gabby was the first one out the door to hop in his jet. This is where the fun started. Gabby got out of the van and we proceeded to the rest of the jets. On the way to the next one the maintenance supervisor flagged us down. He informed us that Frenchy's jet had a hydraulic leak and that he would be flying the spare, which was in the shelter just next door. The only difference between the two was that the new jet didn't have the MK-84's on it. Frenchy jumped out and then Shotgun and I went to our jets.

Since the weather was threatening to go below our minimums, we rushed our ground ops in an effort to get airborne before the weather rolled in. Remember, now, that everybody in the flight, except Gabby, knew that Frenchy's jet didn't have bombs on it.

We took to the runway, launched at 20-second intervals, and immediately we started the "radar trail departure from Hell." We all flew two to four miles behind the preceding aircraft, using our radar to follow behind, and on instruments the whole way. We stayed in radar trail, and in the weather, for a good twenty minutes as we flew east looking for some clear air over the range. Finally, we found VMC (Visual Meteorological Conditions; in other words, no clouds!) between cloud layers at about 12,000 feet. We stayed in trail for a few more minutes since Shotgun wasn't sure if we'd be able to maintain VMC as we flew over the range talking to the FAC. The FAC, of course, cleared us on the range to drop "Hot" despite the fact that he couldn't even see the tops of the mountains due to the weather! We made several radar runs at the range waiting for the slight chance that the weather might break in our lifetime, but to no avail. Even though we probably could have done so fairly accurately, the rules didn't allow us to drop our bombs unless we could actually see the target.

It had now been about 45 minutes since takeoff and despite our valiant efforts, we weren't going to drop our bombs this day. So Shotgun called for a rejoin to 4-ship route formation, which had all four airplanes within a few feet of each other. We rejoined and flew together for several minutes when the fun starts.

Suddenly, over the flight *VHF* radio frequency, came a distressed call from Gabby to Frenchy. "Three, this is four. You don't have a bomb on your right wing!" Frenchy, who is one of the coolest practical jokers of all time, never missed a beat and came back to Gabby with, "REALLY! Check my left wing!" As if he couldn't move his head and look out the bubble canopy at his own left wing! I looked over and I saw Gabby dip his jet down enough so he could see Frenchy's left wing. He flew back up into formation and said frantically, "Three, you don't have one on that wing either!" At this point, I was gasping for air because I was laughing so hard!

All the while this was going on, Shotgun was on *UHF* talking to ATC (Air Traffic Control) and all he heard is that something was missing off of a jet. Shotgun asked Frenchy what the problem was and Frenchy came on the radio and said, "Four, I didn't takeoff with any!" Shotgun was initially slightly behind the conversation that was taking place, but he quickly caught up!

By the time that Gabby realized that the bombs hadn't dropped off of Frenchy's jet, I was crying! I was laughing so hard that I was literally crying and my gut was hurting. I had to drop my mask to wipe my eyes. We managed to land back at Osan without any further crises.

Gabby only endured a slight (NOT!) amount of ribbing from the Samurai buds once we got back in the squadron ops building and related what had happened. There was serious consideration to changing his given Samurai callsign, but he survived the public ridicule with his original Samurai name.

To this day, the incident still makes me laugh out loud. Definitely one of the funniest moments I've ever experienced in the air.[13]

The next pilot I spoke with left the squadron just a short time ago. He is another case of a young guy coming to the squadron right out of pilot training. For some reason, not many people in the Air Force are aware of what a great place Misawa is. They easily get scared off by the horror stories of snow (Misawa averages over 10 feet a year) and are intimidated by the thought of living in Japan. There are, however, plenty of good things to offset the bad, as you will soon learn.

Rabid

They say you'll never love a squadron as much as your first operational fighter squadron. I think that will hold true for me. It has so far but my career is still young. I spent three and a half years with the Samurai. "Ripple" and I were the only two lieutenants to show up in the squadron for more than a year and a half. Ripple got there before I did so I was the Snack-O (snack bar officer, responsible for keeping the fridge full of sodas, beer, and food) for all of 1995 until another lieutenant finally showed up in mid 1996. The squadron was heavy on experience and light on lieutenants. When I hear guys talk about their first fighter squadron, the stories oftentimes revolve around the social aspect of having a bunch of young lieutenants fired up in the air and on the ground. For us, there were only two members in the LPA. The LPA, or Lieutenants Protective Association, was an unofficial group, with the sole purpose being to party together and to get on the nerves of the captains and majors! Now, the Samurai had a good time, like any fighter squadron. It just wasn't fueled by the LPA. When I left things were getting back to some sense of normalcy in that regard. I think there were eight or nine lieutenants then and you started hearing comments again like, "It's a good thing you guys are still lieutenants, but you won't be bulletproof forever. Don't do that again!"

Most of the memories and stories I have about being a Samurai revolve around the places the Samurai took me. I saw the world in three and a half years. We were lucky in PACAF because we weren't supporting the desert deployments for my first two years there. All of our TDYs were two weeks to one month long and they were all training deployments, that is, fun.

One month in Fairbanks, Alaska in June. What a beautiful place in the summer! Twenty four hours of daylight is amazing and has a tendency to wear you out if you don't watch it!

F-16 ready to refuel over Alaska, returning to Misawa. (Joanie Thole)

Two weeks in Medan, Indonesia. A third world country with F-16s! That was by far the most talked-about deployment I went on. Totally unique. I remember that we would cross a bridge over a river everyday on the way to the base. The river was pretty swift and brown as mud. There were always naked kids playing or bathing in it, men fishing in it, women washing clothes and dishes in it, and people using it as a toilet. All of this at the same time, up stream and down stream from each other, it didn't matter.

We got to golf for free there on the military golf course. We just paid for a caddy (one each). You could pay them whatever you wanted so we agreed that we would give them 10,000 Rupia per nine holes. That was less than $5. Word got around fast and when the caddies would see our van pulling up they would mob us, over 50 of them, each trying to get his hands on our golf bags. We called their ringmaster the "Caddy Pimp." If they got too rough he would punch one of them in the mouth and the rest would straighten up. We found out later that we were pissing the Indonesian pilots off because they would only pay them two to three thousand Rupia for 18 holes and we were making them look bad. No wonder we got mobbed.

    A month in Singapore. A stark contrast to Indonesia. We could use Medan as a divert base from there but it was a different world. Very clean and modern. Great food and bars, but expensive, $30 for a pitcher of beer. Everyone talked about our favorite little dive, Stall 40. It was a seafood "hawker" stand. We would sit around the little cement tables and eat barbecued stingray, chili prawns, and chili crab and talk about the day's BFM sorties.

    That was my first year. The next year we spent a month in Vegas and Hill AFB in Utah, for a Green Flag and Combat Hammer deployment. Billeting was at Circus Circus in Vegas. Hurt me. Ripple and I, the only two lieutenants on the trip, were the only two pilots who got to shoot both a live Maverick missile and a live HARM missile. The squadron leadership thought it was more important for the young guys to get to do something like that than for the experienced guys who had already seen a lot in their careers. We didn't complain.

Samurai Block 30s prepare to take the runway at Cope Thunder. (Author)

Then it was off to Alaska again for a month and later, Korea for a month. After that the deployments started to slack off some as Misawa started to pick up the desert rotations. The Samurai picked up Turkey for three months in the spring and summer of 97. We took six jets and seven pilots and it turned out not to be a bad deal at all. We had a blast there. Getting there was somewhat of a chore. We had to fly the long way around the earth to get to Turkey from Japan - east. From Misawa to Eielson AFB, Alaska, to Lajes Air Base in the Azores to Incirlik, Turkey. The second leg, from Alaska to the Azores, is a flight I will always remember. The worst weather I've ever taken off in and the worst weather I've ever landed in with some of the most beautiful sights I've ever seen in between.

We took off at 2 a.m. It had just started snowing when we taxied. When we were ready to take off the snow was coming down pretty hard but tower still said the visibility was three miles. We believed them. After all, we couldn't tell since it was dark. But as we rolled down the runway one by one it became obvious to each of us that the vis was much worst than that. The taxi light reflected off of the big snow flakes so badly that it was all you could do to just keep the jet straight by splitting the distance between each set of runway lights as they came into view one at a time. There was no way we were going to land back there. Soon after we got airborne, the tankers radioed us saying they couldn't take off because the snow was building up on their wings and they had to shut down to de-ice. No problem, we would meet up with them at the first re-fueling point. So we proceeded out over northern Canada to wait.

Every pilot probably has an image in their memory that confirms for them the reason they had to become a pilot. It is that defining moment when you experience what the author of High Flight meant when he said, "Oh I have slipped the surly bonds of earth and danced the skies on laughter silvered wings…and seen a hundred things you have not dreamed of." This was mine.

We broke through the clouds and into the crystal clear night air. The tops of the clouds were dimly lit by starlight. At first I didn't notice much else because I was concentrating on getting rejoined with the rest of the flight. I was number five of six, so my position was one to two miles behind lead's four-ship. My wingman (#6) rejoined on me to a route position, about two ship-widths beside me. Once we were rejoined, there was nothing to do but relax, follow lead and wait for the tankers. And notice my surroundings.

There were more stars out that night than I have ever seen. We were so far out over northern Canada that we couldn't even talk to ATC on the radios any more. No civilization to light the clouds from below. This was April of '97. If you are a sky gazer you will remember that was when the comet Hale-Bopp was visible. I had seen the comet from the ground but never from the air and never without a single light on the ground to wash it out. There it was out the left side of my cockpit. It was immense. Easily the length of a pencil held at arm's length. Then out the right side of the cockpit were the Northern Lights. They were slight but definitely there. Thin green wisps of light slowly dancing on the horizon. "Oh I have slipped the surly bonds of earth."

It was silent for a while out there. You could tell that everyone was kind of mesmerized by it. Until, "Lead, I'm starting to get a little low on gas." That ended the silence. We still hadn't heard anything from the tankers yet and we had been airborne for an hour. Lead started to take us back to Eielson, which generated even more discussion. Some of us didn't think we should be going back to a base that was below mins when we took off (and probably still was if the tankers couldn't get airborne), when we couldn't even talk to anyone on the radio. But before we had to fight out where we were going to go, the tankers came up on the radio and we were able to get rejoined and be on our way.

As we approached the Azores, we began to realize that the one-hour delay was going to affect our arrival. For one, it was going to be very close to sunset, and two, the weather was starting to get steadily worse. The ceiling and visibility came down to the point that we had to break up the formation and each fly our own separate instrument approach. All six of us had the same comment about what it was like to pop out of the weather on that approach. "Did you see that big church on final?" The cross winds were over fifty knots on final approach, so when you popped out of the weather and looked straight ahead to where the runway usually was, there was a big Catholic cathedral instead. It took a couple of seconds to realize that there was so much crab on final to overcome the crosswinds and stay on course that the runway was actually 30 degrees to the right. The crosswinds were only about 25 knots at the surface, which is right on the limit but it made the landing sporty. One guy put his hook down on roll out because he didn't think he was going to get stopped in time. I had to go around and make a second attempt when a gust blew me off the edge of the runway in the flare. But we all made it safely and had a lot to talk about over our swordfish dinner at Pescadore's Seafood restaurant that night. It was my longest flight in the F-16, 11.5 hours.

About halfway through my tour I was fortunate to become the narrator for the PACAF F-16 Demo Team. "Shadow" was the pilot and team leader. The jets we used belonged to the Samurai. We traveled to airshows in Japan and to big international trade shows throughout the Pacific. Shadow and I went all over the place showing off the Viper. I went to five different bases in Japan, plus Seoul, Guam, Singapore, and Melbourne, Australia. It was on the return trip from Melbourne that my most interesting Samurai story took place.

Shadow and I were returning to Misawa from the weeklong 1997 Australian International Air Show. Two F-16s and a KC-135 for air refueling. Since the F-16 is a single engine fighter, you are always keenly aware of where the nearest airfield is in case you have any engine trouble. About halfway through the first leg of our trip (Melbourne to Guam) I experienced engine trouble. The engine transferred into its secondary mode. The computer that runs the engine had failed. In the secondary mode the engine operates like older jet engines did before they had computers. Not a huge problem but a "land at the nearest airfield" kind of a deal, especially when you are 250 miles from land. The nearest airfield was Port Moresby, Papua New Guinea. It had been briefed to us as a suitable airfield in case we couldn't get gas from the tanker for some reason so we saw no reason not to land there. I landed first and they had me park in an empty airliner slot. The first thing I noticed was about 20 or 30 people staring at the jet through the fence, like they had never seen a fighter before. They all had on shorts, some had shirts, some didn't and some were bare foot, others wore sandals. They just kept staring. Shadow joined me shortly and so did the tanker with our maintenance crew. We were soon joined by the Australian attaché. His first words were something to the effect of, "What are you blokes doing here?"

We explained, to which he replied that we didn't want to be here and he had called the American consulate and they were on the way to explain the situation. When they arrived they gave us a current event update on the country we had just landed in. They explained that American embassies are rated on a scale of low, medium, high, and critical for various threats. For instance, Moscow was rated critical for the threat of espionage during the cold war. Of the over 250 embassies and consulates in the world there were only four at the time that were rated critical for the threat of violent crime; Haiti, Mogadishu, Rwanda and of course, Port Moresby, Papua New Guinea! The city was under marshal law after 10 p.m. until sunrise. Apparently there were roving street gangs that would just kill people for the hell of it. Gratuitous killing they called it. You had to have a special pass to be out after dark and government police would shoot first and ask questions later if something looked suspicious. Well, that was enough for the tanker crew. They unloaded our maintenance people and gear and left as soon as they could!

We got set up in a hotel, which was pretty nice actually, and started to figure out how we were going to get home. We needed a new engine flown in for my jet. Seemed like that should be a pretty simple thing. Put one on a plane and have it down here tomorrow. Not so simple. Turns out we had landed at a politically sensitive time. The day prior to our arrival, it had been leaked to the press that the government of New Guinea was planning to hire mercenaries from South Africa to help them fight a civil war they had been fighting for the last few years up on one of their northern islands. The whole international community had publicly condemned them for it, especially Australia and New Zealand. Then the next day two U.S. fighters land, unannounced, in their capital city. The head of the U.S. consulate showed us a communiqué from someone on the Prime Minister's staff to the U.S. State department saying that they didn't believe that the fighters that had landed had any real problem. They resented that we staged an emergency so we could land in their country. They did not appreciate these "strong arm" tactics from the U.S. The C-130 bringing the engine for the F-16 would not be given permission to land as they did not believe there was any real problem. I don't know how far our little predicament made it up the chain of command but I know the commander of PACAF knew about us and so did the State Department. Whether or not the President heard about us in his daily briefs we'll probably never know.

Someone intervened somewhere and our C-130 was allowed to bring in the engine and some security police to relieve us of guard duty. We had to have two people with the airplanes at all times, armed with a cell phone. It was nice to have real security police take over for us but they weren't allowed to bring weapons into the country so they were armed with cell phones too. We ended up staying there three and a half days. As bad as things appeared though, things weren't all that terrible. No one rushed the planes and we never got caught out after dark. We spent our time with the jets, in the hotel or in the consulate.

Had Shadow and I known what our next assignment was going to be we would have spent a lot more time shopping. Both of us went to Kunsan Air Base in South Korea, he a Juvat and I a Panton. Both squadrons' World War II history centers around their time flying out of Port Moresby. That's why the 80th (Juvats) are known as the Head Hunters. Maybe we could have found some WWII artifacts in some antique shop. Oh well. I'm sure we were the first U.S. fighters to land there since World War II. Some weeks later we read in the papers that the government of Papua New Guinea had decided against hiring the mercenaries. Shadow and I joked: mission accomplished![14]

As I mentioned earlier, flying fighters is indeed a high risk proposition. The danger doesn't go away just because we are not at war. Accidents happen in training, and American fighter pilots are being shot at daily as this is written in such desolate places as Iraq and the former Yugoslavia. Training for these missions is just as dangerous.

Reefer

I arrived at Misawa in the middle of June '98, about three or four weeks behind Ronin. Lt. Brice "Ronin" Simpson and his wife Katie had been good friends of mine since pilot training. The fact that he chose Misawa for his first duty assignment played a major factor in my own decision for Misawa. I had brief encounters with him at the Air Force Academy, but it wasn't until pilot training that I really got to know him well. He was in the class immediately in front of me at pilot training, Introduction to Fighter Fundamentals (IFF, the new politically correct name for LIFT), and RTU.

Block 30 F-16 approaching the departure end of runway 10. (Author)

During one of his initial training rides, in August I think it was, he aborted his takeoff at or near refusal speed. He was unable to stop the jet and ended up running off the end of the overrun. Just prior to departing the prepared surface, he ejected and landed within 50 feet (probably closer) to his F-16, which of course had erupted into flames. One American staff sergeant, who was driving around the airfield perimeter, and three Japanese joggers witnessed the crash. Ronin had become tangled in the parachute lines and they immediately responded by trying to pull him from the flames. At first they were unsuccessful due to the extreme heat generated by the burning F-16. On the second attempt they were able to pull him from the flames and put out the fire that was burning his legs. By this time the firefighters had shown up, and were putting out the fire. They put him in an ambulance and rushed him to the hospital.

At the hospital, I was able to see him a couple times from a distance as they moved him from room to room. It was amazing that he was still alive, judging by his looks. He was then sent to Brooks (a military hospital in the States) on a specially configured C-141 that had to fly at low altitude so that he would not burst with the decrease in pressure. There he fought a battle for his life that lasted for almost a full two months. In the end he succumbed to the infection. His funeral was held at the USAF Academy with full military honors and a missing man formation of Vipers flown by his former squadron from Luke AFB.

Fighter pilots today typically aren't given their callsign until after they have finished their initial training at their first operational base. We made an exception for Brice while he was at Brooks. There were only a couple of

Samurai around Misawa at the time because the rest of the squadron was blowing sand in Saudi Arabia. We finally came up with "Ronin." The Ronin were a class of Samurai that went on their own and were generally left to fend for themselves. We felt that this was appropriate due to the fact that he was battling for his life in San Antonio without any Samurai in a 3,000 mile radius. His name was put on the canopy of one of our jets, tail number 919.

The Samurai deployed to Saudi Arabia in support of Operation Southern Watch (*OSW*) in March of 1999 for a 45-day tour that got extended to 90 days. On my very first sortie I was flying with the ViceWing Commander. We were assigned to the far western side of Iraq for our SEAD orbit. We would orbit and keep an eye on the Iraqi SAM sites while scores of other U.S., British, and French aircraft patrolled the area for Iraqi air and ground targets. In the past few days, the Iraqis had moved some of their SAM sites and at this point some were still "missing." While heading east towards one of these "unlocated" SA-2 sites, I detected the site on my HTS display. I called it out to my flight lead and he initiated a turn towards the south. At that point I received a missile guidance indication on my RWR. I called it out as cool as I could and began to maneuver to determine if I was indeed targeted. The visibility that day was outstanding as long as you were above 10,000 feet. Below that, however, there was a whole lot of blowing sand. You could only see ground features that were directly below your jet. Even roads were difficult to make out. After about 15 seconds of solid missile launch indications I still hadn't seen a missile launch and had to assume the worst. I called out on the radio what I was doing and started a maneuver that we are taught will defeat an SA-2. After a total of 83 seconds I was able to break the lock of the SA-2. Later on in the deployment we learned that the SAM sites hadn't moved a great distance when they went "unlocated" and I was in fact outside the SA-2's max range the entire time. Needless to say I was a little nervous, this being my first "combat" sortie.

Reefer pulls into the End of Runway area at Misawa. (USAF)

We saw AAA on about a third or a quarter of our sorties. I personally witnessed AAA on four different occasions. Only once was it anywhere close. "B-squared," our squadron commander at the time, and I were flying past Tallil with two Eagles at our 9 o'clock high for about three to four miles when AAA started bursting all around them.

After talking to the pilots later, they said that there were four bursts that blew up between their two jets. This was before we were carrying Mavericks so there really wasn't anything that we could do about it. The Samurai provided SEAD coverage for approximately ten different strikes on Iraq during the various presidentially-mandated airstrikes that summer.

One significant event while we were there occurred on 28 May 1999. It was three days before the LPA pinned on captain. We had all graduated the Academy the same day, so our promotions would all be simultaneous. "Chewie" and I were flying together, both of us lieutenants. "Screamin" was leading another two-ship of Samurai. One of the tankers fell out, and half of the assets were sent back to land. As it turned out Screamin went home early for some reason or another, leaving the LPA as the only force protection assets in the entire "no fly" zone, alone and unafraid!

Since then the 14th has had a PACAF Combat Employment Readiness Inspection (CERI, the new politically correct name for an ORI). We received an excellent rating, literally with no help from the Panthers.[15]

Warren "Reefer" Sneed and his wife Nancy at Misawa (Sneed)

As a very sad footnote to Reefer's story, as this book was being written Captain Warren "Reefer" Sneed was killed in a mid-air collision while flying a training sortie off of the west coast of Japan. As of this writing, his body has not been found. There were conflicting reports as to whether or not he was able to eject from his aircraft and after several days of searching, the effort was called off and he was pronounced dead.

Notes

1. - Sluggo to Author, letter, subject: 14th TFS history, 14 October 1999.

2. - Dano to Author, letter, subject: 14th TFS history, 14 December 1999.

3. - Smokin, interviewed by Author, 14 September 1999.

4. - Ibid.

5. - Ibid.

6. - Ibid.

7. - Ibid.

8. - Ibid.

9. - Ibid.

10. - Ibid.

11. - Ibid.

12. - Ibid.

13. - Merge to Author, letter, subject: 14th TFS history, 10 December 1999.

14. - Rabid to Author, letter, subject: 14th TFS history, 14 November 1999.

15. - Reefer to Author, letter, subject: 14th TFS history, 27 December 1999.

About the Author

The author is an F-16 pilot in the United States Air Force. He flew with the 14th Fighter Squadron in the early 1990's and has since served operational tours in Korea and the United States. He has nearly 2000 hours in the F-16.

APPENDIX

Additional Information on the 14th

For those of you who can remember way back to the introduction, recall that I said you were in the wrong place if you were looking for facts and figures. If you still want those facts and figures, I have included a list of books and periodicals which contain information on the 14th or pictures of its airplanes. This is by no means an exhaustive list, but a listing of the books and magazines I have acquired in the course of my research on the squadron. For the books, I have included information on where to purchase them and if they are out of print. For the periodicals, I have included the publisher so you can contact them to see if they still have any copies. Otherwise, your best bet is to scour the used book market and see what you can find. All of the information below is current as of March 2000. Happy hunting.

Museums

USAF Museum, Dayton Ohio.

Besides being the finest aviation museum in the United States, the USAF Museum has an RF-4C on display as well as a Spitfire Mk. XI. What is unique about the Spitfire is that it is painted in the colors of the 14th PRS. The only other museum I have seen that rivals this one is the Naval Aviation Museum in Pensacola, Florida. I like these museums better than the Smithsonian because you can get up close and personal with the aircraft, to touch and walk under and around many of them. If you have a computer and Internet access, you can log onto www.wpafb.af.mil/museum/air_power/ap17.htm for a picture of the Spitfire.

Books

Boyne, Walter J., *Phantom in Combat.* Atglen, PA.: Shiffer Publishing, 1994.

This 176 page, hardcover book takes a look at the Phantom from inception to its use by the Israelis in the Bekka valley. Of the books mentioned in this list, this one has the most first-hand accounts, concentrating heavily on air-to-air combat. If you want to get a feel for the nitty-gritty of fighting in the Phantom, this is the one. There are only a couple of pictures of the 14th, although there are quite a few photos taken by RF-4s, without the squadron being identified. See Amazon.com to order as this book is still in print.

Drendel, Lou. *U.S.A.F. Phantoms in Combat.* Carrolton, TX.: Squadron/Signal, 1987.

This 63 page, paperback book has only one photo of a 14th RF-4 but is filled with great pictures and stories from pilots and WSOs who flew the Phantom in Vietnam. Although out of print, Amazon.com offers to search for the book to see if any copies are available.

Ethell, Jeffrey L., and Robert T. Sand. *Fighter Command: American Fighters in Original WW II Color.* Osceola, WI.: Motorbooks International, 1991.

This hardcover book is 176 pages of color photographs and first-person accounts of flying fighters over Europe in WW II. While only one short chapter (six pages) is devoted to reconnaissance, several pilots give their accounts, one from the 14th which is partially quoted in the work you just read. Most of the pictures are of the P-38 photo variants. The photos are not labeled by squadron, but the aircraft certainly could have belonged to the 14th. I highly recommend this book for its many great stories of flying piston-engine fighters and the great photographs. It is available from Amazon.com and is currently in print.

Keen, Patricia Fussel. *Eyes of the Eighth: A Story of the 7th Photographic Reconnaissance Group, 1942-1945.* Sun City, AZ.: CAVU Publishers, 1996

If you are still looking for those facts and figures on the WW II activities of the 14th, this is the place to stop. This hardcover book is a monster, 378 pages total, and very detailed. The book draws heavily from the daily combat reports of the 7th Photographic Reconnaissance Group and delivers a day-by-day account of the group's activities. The 14th plays a prominent role in the book and there are many fine photographs as well. This book is available directly from the distributor at Pathway Book Service, 4 White Brook Road, Gilsum, NH 03448; Ph: 603-357 0236 Fax: 603 -357 2073 or http://www.pathwaybook.com. It can also be obtained by special order from Barnes and Noble at BN.com.

Kinzey, Bert, and Ray Leader. *Colors and Markings.* Vol. 23, *Colors and Markings of the Recon Phantoms.* Waukesha, WI.: Kalmbach Publishing, 1994.

    This is volume 23 of the popular *Colors and Markings* series. Primarily designed for aircraft modelers, the book is full of color and black and white photographs. There is only one photo of a 14th jet, but it is one of the few in print to show the "Playboy Bunny" on the intake. Because it was designed for modelers, there is little text other than the captions and very little technical detail. The book is currently out of print but Amazon.com offers it as a special order.

Lake, John. *McDonnell F-4 Phantom: Spirit in the Skies.* Westport, CT.: Airtime Publishing, 1992.

    This book is a 232 page, hardcover history of the mighty Phantom. Produced by the folks at the *World Airpower Journal*, the book has many full color photographs and a few first-hand accounts of flying and fighting in the Phantom. Like most books on the Phantom, reconnaissance is not given a prominent part and there are only a few pictures of the 14th, with one sidebar devoted to a particularly hairy mission tasked with post-strike photos of the Paul Doumer bridge. This book is still in print and available from Amazon.com.

Miller, Jay. *Aerofax Minigraph 13, McDonnell RF-4 Variants.* Osceola, WI.: Motorbooks International, 1984.

    This is a thin, paperback book jam-packed with photos and information on the RF-4. There is only one photo of a 14th RF-4, but there are plenty of detailed photos of the cockpit and systems of the RF-4. The first few pages contain a detailed description of the history, development, and specifications of the jet. This book is available from Amazon.com and is currently in print. If you want specifications and details about the RF-4, without much narrative, this is the book for you.

Thornborough, Anthony M., and Peter E. Davies. *The Phantom Story.* London, UK.:Arms and Armour Press, 1994.

Of the books mentioned here, this hardcover, 288 page book gives the RF-4 the most coverage, devoting 40 pages to reconnaissance. The 14th is rarely mentioned, but you do get a real nice feel for the mission of reconnaissance and the systems involved as well as a look at how the RF-4 has fared since the end of the Vietnam War. This book does a nice job of covering the Phantom's history all the way through the Gulf War and covers the RAF Phantoms in good detail. Although out of print, Amazon.com offers it as a special order.

Periodicals

"432d Fighter Wing, Misawa." *Koku-Fan Illustrated* 93-6, No., 70.

This will be a tough one to get hold of, but probably the best of the bunch for pictures of the 14th TFS at Misawa. There are over 50 pages of text and full-color photos, mostly of the 14th with a few disappointing pictures of the 13th. I would give you the publishing information, but I bought this book in Japan and all of the text is in Japanese! They may have published an English language version, but I can't tell you for sure. If you do a little digging at some of the aviation book companies you may be able to scare up a copy. The photos are outstanding and if you don't mind doing a little digging, I think any fan of F-16s and the 14th in particular will find it worthwhile.

Adams, Gerald. "Strange Encounter of a Recce Pilot and a Komet." *Friend's Journal* 16, No. 3 (Fall 1993): 29-31.

Published for members of the Air Force Museum Foundation, this volume contains the complete text of Gerald Adams' encounter with a Me-163 while flying with the 14th PRS. Included are a couple of photographs of the Me-163 and a squadron photo taken in 1945. Also included are the author's attempts to find the German pilot he encountered that day. The foundation can be contacted at P.O. Box 1903, Wright-Patterson AFB, OH 45433-1903 or www.intecon.com/museum.

Martin, Patrick. "Dead Phantoms- RF-4C Losses in Southeast Asia." *Smoke Trails: Quarterly Journal of the Phantom II Society* 8, No., 2: 9-11.

This issue has an article devoted to all USAF RF-4C losses during the Vietnam War. It lists each jet lost by tail number and reason. Four photos of 14th jets are included. Contact the society at P.O. Box 900174, San Diego CA 92190-0174 or (858) 689-9227 from 8 a.m. to 4 p.m. Pacific Time to inquire about back issues.

"Misawa's Weasels." *Air Force Magazine* 82, No. 9 (September 1999): 56-63.

This issue, published as always by the Air Force Association, features an eight-page, color layout of the F-16s at Misawa. Although you will have to suffer through some pictures of 13th TFS jets, you can easily dismiss them and concentrate on the ones with the yellow fin flashes. This is a nice look at Misawa and the current equipment of the Samurai. Contact the Air Force Association at 1501 Lee Highway, Allington VA 22209-1198 or phone (703) 247-5800.

O'Leary, Michael. "Yankee Spy Spitfires." *Air Classics* 29, No. 7 (July 1993): 35-47.

This issue details the restoration of the Spitfire Mk. XI currently on display at the USAF Museum. Along with a brief history of the model, there are lots of nice photographs, some in color, and a few of the cockpit. This magazine can be found in just about any bookstore, and there is usually information about ordering back issues as well as advertisements for numerous aviation book companies inside.

"PACAF Power." *World Airpower Journal* 14 (Fall 1993): 138-147.

This quarterly journal is published in the U.K. and is an excellent source of photographs and information regarding modern aviation. This particular issue has a ten-page spread on the Pacific Air Forces, with one page on Misawa. The price of the book may be a bit steep for one page of photographs, but if you are interested you can contact the publisher at www.airpower.co.uk.

Glossary

AB: Afterburner. This is a way to increase the thrust of a jet engine by pouring fuel into the exhaust of the engine and igniting it. This also doubles or triples the amount of fuel used. An F-16 in full afterburner will exhaust all of its internal fuel in about 10 minutes!

ACM: Air Combat Maneuvering. This type of air-to-air training typically pits two aircraft, which are designated as "blue" fighters (the good guys), against one bandit (the bad guy). This can be from a pre-arranged setup where the single bandit starts behind the two-ship (a defensive setup for the blue fighters) or in front of the blue fighters (an offensive setup for the blue fighters). Often, the blue fighters simply orbit in the center of the training area, and the bandit makes random attacks on the element. This training is designed to give the fighters practice with visual lookout, defensive reactions, and two-ship coordination.

ACT: Air Combat Tactics. A less scripted air-to-air training scenario pitting two or more fighters against two or more bandits. When this training is flown against another type of aircraft, it is referred to as Dissimilar Air Combat Tactics, or DACT.

ADO: Assistant Operations Officer. This officer is typically third in the chain of command in a fighter squadron, following the commander and the operations officer.

AFB: Air Force Base. Bases in the U.S. are known as air force bases, whereas bases overseas are commonly referred to as air bases.

AGL/MSL: Above Ground Level/Mean Sea Level. Pilots use two different types of altitude to describe how high they are. If a pilot is flying 1,000 feet over the airfield at the Air Force Academy in Colorado, he is 1,000 feet AGL, but at the same time he is approximately 7,500 feet MSL, or above Mean Sea Level. The elevation of the airfield is approximately 6,500 feet MSL. If you stand at the top of Pikes Peak in Colorado Springs, Colorado, you are at 0 feet AGL but will be over 14,000 feet MSL.

AIM-120 (AMRAAM): This is a radar guided missile carried by most U.S. fighters. It was introduced into the F-16 fleet in the early 1990's. This is considered a Beyond Visual Range (BVR) weapon, as it can be fired at targets well outside of visual range. You can typically see a fighter-sized target out to around five miles, while a target like an F-15 can be easily seen out to eight miles or more.

AIM-9 (Sidewinder): This shorter ranged, infra-red guided missile is carried by the F-16 and all other U.S. fighters. It is sometimes referred to as a "heat seeker."

Air evac: Aerial evacuation.

BFM: Basic Fighter Maneuvers. This is a general term for air-to-air training pitting one fighter against another. These fights usually start out with one fighter on the offense and one on the defense. The objective is for the offensive fighter to shoot down the defensive fighter in the shortest amount of time possible. Normally, one of the fighters will be designated as the training aid, having to replicate the maneuvers or weapons of a threat aircraft, such as a MiG-29 Fulcrum. If the offensive fighter is the training aid, the objective of the defensive fighter will be to survive any attacks by the offender and to capitalize on any of his mistakes. A building block approach to training a new fighter pilot will start out with BFM, progress to ACM, and finally finish up with ACT.

Bingo: a game played by little old ladies and the 13th Fighter Squadron or a codeword meaning "I'm getting low on fuel."

Boosted ailerons: The controls of most airplanes during World War II were moved by cables, rods, and pulleys. As the speed of the airplane increased, the wind resistance against the control surfaces made it extremely difficult to maneuver the airplane. The Lockheed P-38 was one of the first airplanes to use hydraulics to boost the controls, similar to installing power steering on a car originally designed with manual steering.

BUFF: Big Ugly Fat Fellow, a nickname for the Boeing B-52 Stratofortress.

CAS: Close Air Support. Bombing missions flown in support of our Army and Marine brothers on the ground. Fighters on CAS missions function like remote controlled artillery for the ground troops, providing extra firepower when they are beyond the support range of their own heavy weapons.

Ceiling: A term to designate the height of the clouds above the ground. If the base of the clouds is at 2,000 feet AGL, then the ceiling is 2,000 feet. "Ceiling" also refers to the maximum altitude an aircraft is capable of reaching in level flight.

Clock positions: Pilots use clock positions to describe where something is in relation to the airplane. If something is straight ahead, it is referred to as being at 12 o'clock. A bandit spotted behind and slightly to the left would be at 7 o'clock.

Combat Hammer: An exercise where operational fighter squadrons get to drop live munitions and shoot air-to-ground missiles. The reliability and effectiveness of the weapons and the pilots are tracked so the USAF can monitor the performance of its weapons and pilots.

Combat SAGE: An exercise similar to Combat Hammer, but conducted in the Philippines.

Cope Thunder: This exercise, along with Red Flag, is designed to give a fighter pilot experience flying in large missions against very robust threats. Studies conducted during the Vietnam War concluded that a fighter pilot's chances of surviving his tour in a war zone rise dramatically after his first ten missions. This exercise is designed to give each pilot those first ten missions in a very stressful, though not deadly, environment. A typical mission will involve up to 60 airplanes of all types trying to attack a target defended by 12 or more adversaries and numerous SAMs and AAA. Very detailed debriefings are held to determine what was done right, and what was done poorly. Cope Thunder was originally held in the Philippines, although after Clark AB was wiped out by a volcano in the early 90's, the exercise was moved to Alaska.

Cruise climb: In many cases, for a fighter pilot, the higher he can fly, the better. But, when heavy with fuel, the airplane will not climb as high as the pilot may desire. Cruise climb is a technique where the pilot will climb as high as the airplane will let him and as fuel burns off, he will then climb higher. This provides a flight path similar to climbing a flight of stairs.

DCO: Deputy Commander for Operations. Under the old wing structure, the commander had various deputies. Operations, logistics, maintenance, supply, etc. The DCO was directly responsible for the flying operations of the wing and was the link in the chain of command between the wing commander and the squadron commander. The organization of the wing is similar today, although it is broken into Groups. The current title for the old DCO is the operations group commander, or OG.

DO: Director of Operations, essentially, the second in command of a fighter squadron. The DO is referred to today as the operations (or ops) officer.

Dollar Ride: In pilot training, a student's first flight is mainly for familiarization, with the IP doing a lot of the flying. There isn't much pressure on the student and it is probably the only ride in pilot training conducted mainly for fun. After this ride, it is tradition for the student to give his IP a dollar.

E-squared presentation: Most radar scopes show a view from above, sometimes referred to as a "God's eye" view. In aircraft with a terrain following radar, such as the RF-4, F-16 Block 40, and the F-15E, the pilot or WSO is provided with a side view of the terrain ahead of the aircraft. This side view is called an E-squared presentation.

Executive Officer: In the USAF, the executive officer is a non-flying, low ranking assistant to the commander. In the Navy, the executive officer (or XO) is analogous to the DO in the Air Force.

FAC: Forward Air Controller. This is an Air Force person, either a pilot on the ground that travels with the Army or a pilot in an airplane who is in contact with the Army units. The FAC is the director of the air war directly overhead the Army. When the Army needs air support, they call the FAC who calls and directs strikes from fighters. The FAC normally marks targets by firing phosphorous rockets at the target so the fighters can find it. Because the ballistics on the rockets aren't that great, it is common for a FAC to radio the fighters, "See my smoke? Put your bombs 100 meters to the north." The FAC is responsible for knowing the positions of the friendly forces on the ground to prevent the fighters from hitting the wrong target.

Forward sector scan: A type of radar display that displays the picture in front of the aircraft. In large aircraft, such as bombers and tankers, the radar sweeps in a complete circle, giving a view ahead, to the side, and behind the aircraft. In a fighter, the radar antenna is in the nose of the airplane and typically only sweeps 60 degrees to the left and right. This means that anything to the side or behind the fighter will not be picked up on radar.

G: The force of gravity. Sitting or standing still, you are experiencing one G. Just as you are forced to the side of a car when it turns, so too is a pilot pushed down in his seat when he turns. Because fighters fly so fast and turn so hard, they can pull as many as nine Gs in a turn. In practical terms, this means that in a nine-G turn a pilot will weigh nine times his normal body weight. When pulling Gs, it is very difficult to move your arms and head, you have a hard time breathing because your diaphragm weighs so much, and the blood in your body is drawn away from your brain and into your arms and legs. If no precautions are taken, your brain runs out of oxygen and you will pass out after about four seconds. Most people can pull about four Gs before they would pass out. The G-suit that fighter pilots wear squeezes the legs and abdomen, making it possible to pull one or two extra Gs. By tightening the muscles in your arms and legs, and by breathing with a certain technique, you can increase your G tolerance by another two to three Gs. The inclined seat in the F-16 can increase your tolerance by another G or so. By straining and by wearing the G-suit, a fighter pilot can withstand nine Gs for a short period. This is all very tiring and requires the pilots to be in reasonable shape.

GCA: Ground Controlled Approach. A GCA is one of several ways for an aircraft to find the runway when the weather is bad. A radar controller sitting on the ground directs the pilot when to turn and when to descend in order to line up with the runway.

GCI: Ground Controlled Intercept. Because of the forward sector scan of fighter radars, they do not always see the "big picture." When fighting, pilots team up with GCI controllers who sit at radar screens with a full 360 degrees of coverage. The controllers can be airborne in an AWACS airplane or on the ground. The two systems, GCI and the fighter radars, complement each other well.

GPS: Global Positioning System. See LORAN.

Groundloop: When the driver of a car loses control, the car can skid sideways and sometimes even do a complete spin. The same thing happens to airplanes when the pilot is unable to keep it going straight after landing or on takeoff. This spin is called a groundloop. These happen much more often in airplanes with a tailwheel. Aircraft with tricycle gear (with a nosegear in front) are not as prone to groundlooping.

Guard: A radio frequency reserved for emergency use. Most fighters flying today have two or more radios, and one is always tuned to Guard frequency in order to hear any distress calls.

HARM: High Speed Anti-Radiation Missile. Technically known as the AGM-88, the HARM is designed to follow the radar beam put out by an enemy SAM.

HF: High Frequency. A set of radio frequencies used to communicate over long distances.

Homeplate: A codeword for a pilot's home airfield.

ID: Identify. One of the hardest aspects of being a fighter pilot is differentiating the good guys from the bad guys. Even with all of the technology available in the 1990s, fighter pilots often have to devise complex tactics to get close enough to a target to identify it before shooting at it. This is especially crucial when working with a FAC or doing CAS.

IFF: Identification, Friend or Foe. Aircraft carry many devices to broadcast to the world their identity and to attempt to verify the identity of others. These systems are generically known as IFF. In the civilian world, these are referred to as transponders. When looking at a blip on a radar screen, everybody looks the same! The IFF puts a code next to the blip, making it easier to identify.

ILS: Instrument Landing System. A system installed at most large airports to allow planes to land when the weather is bad. Radio signals are broadcast outward from the end of a runway, and the pilot has a display in the cockpit that allows him to line up on the signal. If flown properly, the ILS will guide him to a landing. The difference between this and a GCA is that the pilot has no displays in the cockpit during a GCA, only the verbal directions given by the controller.

INS: Inertial Navigation System. The INS is a self-contained navigation unit inside the aircraft. A typical INS is comprised of three gyros, spinning at high speed. Just as a child's top resists being pushed while it is spinning, so too do the gyros in an INS. After engine start, the pilot will turn on the INS and will tell the computer the current latitude, longitude, and elevation. Every time the aircraft turns, climbs, dives, or accelerates the forces push on the gyros and the computer measures the forces. The computer adds these changes to the starting position to calculate a new, current position for the aircraft.

IP: Depending on the context, either Initial Point or Instructor Pilot. For bombing and reccie runs, the navigation point prior to the target is called the IP. This is an easily recognizable point from which to begin the final attack run.

Jink: A violent, unpredictable maneuver pilots use to dodge enemy bullets and missiles.

LOC: Line of Communication. Military jargon for a road!

LORAN: LOng RAnge Navigation. This system of navigation was designed for ships and adapted for aviation use. Radio stations are set up throughout an area and a receiver on the ship/aircraft receives the signals. Since each station sends out a unique signal, the receiver can triangulate the incoming signals and determine the current position. Today's Global Positioning System (GPS) works the same way, except the radio stations are on satellites.

Maverick: Technically the AGM-65, this is an air-to-ground missile designed primarily to kill tanks. The missile is equipped with either a television or infra-red seeker and provides a picture to the pilot in the cockpit. The pilot ID's the target, locks the missile onto it, and shoots. Later versions of the Maverick are excellent anti-ship weapons.

Mil Power: Military power. Mil power is the maximum power of the engine without using afterburner.

Oblique cameras: Cameras mounted in the aircraft in such a way that they look sideways.

ONW: Operation Northern Watch. This is one of two taskings the USAF has in order to enforce the "no-fly" zones established in Iraq after the Gulf

War. Pilots absolutely hate going on these deployments. They last anywhere from three to five months and are spent in some rather unpleasant places. ONW pilots are based out of Turkey. The missions are very boring and politically driven. The Iraqis still shoot back, but political concerns keep our fighter pilots from effectively defending themselves. Recently, our pilots have been ordered to drop concrete filled bombs in order to minimize "collateral damage!"

OSW: Operation Southern Watch. This is the operation to enforce the "no fly" zone in southern Iraq. It was the troops working OSW that were attacked in the 1996 Khobar Towers bombing. When a unit returns from an ONW or OSW tour, they are typically not fit for combat as the demands of the mission do not allow the types of training necessary to keep a fighter pilot proficient. It takes upwards of a month to re-train the squadron and to recover from a tour in the desert. The living conditions in Saudi Arabia are what you would imagine them to be and the restrictions placed on our service men and women are unbelievable. No one is allowed to drink alcohol in deference to our Saudi "hosts," although the French and British governments for awhile did not impose this restriction on their own troops in theater. Women cannot go off base alone and must wear the dress of the local women, completely covering the body, from head to toe. Women cannot drive a car outside of the base, and more alarmingly, when Sadaam Hussein does something to defy the UN sanctions, the Saudis refuse permission to strike back. Any fighter pilot that chaffed under the ludicrous rules and restrictions during the Vietnam War would immediately recognize what is happening in Southwest Asia. It is these two operations which, in this author's opinion, are single-handedly responsible for driving American fighter pilots out of the Air Force in droves.

Ops officer: Operations Officer. See DO.

Paveway: The nickname given to a class of laser-guided bombs. These bombs were developed during Vietnam and still play an important role today. They are the most accurate air-to-ground weapons ever fielded. An aircraft finds the target and shines a high powered laser on it. The bomb, dropped from another aircraft or from the same one that has the laser, is able to guide on the laser beam to the target.

Phase I/Phase II inspection: Major inspections are broken into two categories. During a Phase I inspection, the unit is evaluated on its ability to get ready for war. Getting the right number of airplanes ready, loaded, and delivered to the fighting location are the major areas graded. The unit's ability to fight is evaluated during a Phase II inspection. Not much flying goes on during a Phase I, as the maintenance troops are the ones doing most of the work. During a Phase II, each pilot flies two to three times a day, and the maintainers still work like crazy to support this frantic pace.

RAF: Royal Air Force. The air arm of the United Kingdom's military.

Recce, Reccie, Recon, Photo Recon, and Photo Reccie: Various ways of saying "reconnaissance" or "photographic reconnaissance." Fighter pilots use these terms because "reconnaissance" is too hard to spell and too hard to say!

Red Crown: Radio callsign for the Navy GCI controllers during the Vietnam War. Red Crown was a boat off the coast of North Vietnam and Disco was the Air Force GCI flying an EC-121 in Laos. The controllers monitored the enemy radio communication as well, and could pass information to the US pilots such as, "They're arming their missiles!"

Red Flag: See Cope Thunder. Red Flag is flown out of Nellis AFB in Nevada.

RHAW/RWR: Radar Homing and Warning/Radar Warning Receiver. Fighters are equipped with instruments telling the pilots when they are being targeted by another radar. This is a very fancy version of the radar detector you can buy for your car.

SARCAP: Search and Rescue Combat Air Patrol. The US Navy pioneered the term Combat Air Patrol (CAP) and it has been adopted by the USAF.

Sawadee: The Thai word for "goodbye."

SOF: Supervisor of Flying. At all U.S. airfields, whenever fighters are flying there is a fighter pilot sitting in the control tower as SOF. He is there to assist the crews in event of an emergency and also to keep an eye on the weather and conditions at the airfield. He is in direct contact with the flying squadrons and the leadership at the base.

Sparrow: A medium ranged, radar-guided missile. Known as the AIM-7, it is the precursor to the AIM-120 AMRAAM.

TACAN: TACtical Air Navigation. This is the system military aircraft use to navigate when the weather prevents them from seeing the ground. Thousands of TACAN stations are installed around the world, broadcasting radio signals for navigation. Instruments in the aircraft display the bearing and range to the selected station.

TDY: Temporary Duty. Military jargon for a business trip!

The Zoo: A nickname for the US Air Force Academy in Colorado Springs. Sometimes used with affection, although rarely!

UHF: Ultra-High Frequency. The set of frequencies used primarily for military communications.

USAAF: United States Army Air Force, formerly known as the United States Army Air Corp and now called the United States Air Force (USAF).

VHF: Very-high Frequency. The set of frequencies most commonly used for aviation communication, both military and civilian.

WSO (RSO, PSO): Weapons System Officer, the official name for the backseater in the F/RF-4. Originally, pilots were used as backseaters, and they were called Pilot Systems Officers. They would serve part of their tour in the rear cockpit, and then upgrade to the front seat. In some platforms, such as the SR-71, the backseater is called a Reconnaissance System Officer. You will sometimes find the backseater in the RF-4 referred to as such.

Weather ship: Sometimes, the first aircraft of the day is launched to check the weather on the way to and in the target area. The need for this duty is less today with the ready availability of satellite weather photos.

Zoomie U: See "The Zoo."

ZPU: Generic name for a small caliber, automatic anti-aircraft artillery gun.

Printed in the United States
2629